Introductory Book to Dr. Ollendorff's New Method of Learning to Write, Read, and Speak a Language in Six Months, Adapted to the Latin

L'auteur et les éditeurs de cet ouvrage se réservent le droit de le traduire ou de le faire traduire en toutes les langues. Ils poursuivront, en vertu des lois, décrets et traités internationaux, toutes contrefaçons ou toutes traductions faites au mépris de leurs droits.

Le dépôt légal de ce volume a été fait à Paris, au Ministère de l'intérieur, dans le cours du mois de juin 1862, et toutes les formalités prescrites par les traités seront remplies dans les divers États avec lesquels la France a conclu des conventions littéraires.

[Each copy has its number and the Author's signature.]

Nº 177.

PREFACE.

THE success which the Treatise on the German Declensions has met with, and the desire expressed by numerous friends of possessing a similar work for Latin, have induced the Author to publish, as an Introduction to his Latin Method, a Treatise on the Latin Declensions. Constant observation and experience in tuition have convinced him of the possibility of reducing this important branch of grammar to practice by means of rules which may be understood at the first perusal.

As in the case of the German declension, the grammarians who have written on this subject have not given students any general rule for discovering at once the declension of a noun, when it presents itself. The five declensions are doubtless a very ingenious help to persons who know how to decline

the nouns; but they rather tend to embarrass be-
ginners, who are thus prevented from regarding the
words of the language as a whole. They are also an
obstacle to the liberty, so valuable to every student,
of applying to what he learns his own mental
powers. Moreover, with very few exceptions, are
we not obliged to remember the genitive case of
each noun to know the declension to which it belongs?

If any person, freeing himself from preconceived
notions, will give the matter but a slight degree of
attention, he will come to the same conclusion as
the Author, namely, that most pupils improve very
slowly in the Latin language, and often give it up
altogether, for no other reason than the disgust
occasioned by the great complication caused by the
classification of the five declensions.

It was therefore necessary to find a way of teach-
ing the Latin declension without fatiguing the
pupil's attention too much, and of classifying the
nouns so that their declension may be easily recog-
nized. This treatise gives for each gender but one
declension, modified and explained, so as to make it
easily understood and retained. The pupil has not

to think of the genitive when he declines a noun; it is the gender which informs him of the declension, a proceeding more natural and more in accordance with our usage in modern languages[1]. Thus, if the pupil wishes to know how to decline *dominus* and *leo*, he need only remember that they are masculine to know that they belong to the masculine declension. If he has to decline such nouns as *mensa* and *ratio*, he will know at once that, being feminine, they are declined according to the declension of feminine nouns. Further, if he has to decline such nouns as *bellum* and *templum*, he will at once discover that, being neuter, they are declined according to the neuter declension. The exceptions alone remain: I have given them all according to the declension of each gender. Lastly, and to complete the declension of the nouns, the rules for the genders are given. The pupil, as he studies them, will become better grounded in the declension: these rules necessarily

---

[1] However, to neglect nothing that may be of any use, and to elucidate the knowledge of the Latin declension in accordance with the ancient manner of recognising the declension of a noun by its genitive, I have added as an appendix to the declension of substantives a table of classification, and a review of the nouns having *is* in the genitive case singular. (See p. 48, et seqq.)

refer to what precedes, and oblige the student to compare the one with the other, which will conribute to fix the declension more firmly in the memory.

Like the Treatise on the German Declensions, this Treatise is but an extract from a complete Method for learning Latin which will soon be published, with the object of enabling students to speak that language like a modern one. May this new work add another benefit to those which I have already bestowed on tuition, and deserve the attention of masters, as well as the approbation which public opinion has hitherto granted me!

A TREATISE

LATIN DECLENSION.

CHAPTER I.

DECLENSION OF SUBSTANTIVES.

Preliminary Rules.

A. All substantives, without exception, have the dative plural ending in *s*.

B. All substantives, without exception, have the genitive plural ending in *um*.

C. All neuter substantives have three cases ending alike, both singular and plural, viz. the nominative, accusative, and vocative.

D. Masculine and feminine substantives have the accusative ending in *m*.

E. The vocative plural is always like the nominative.

F. All masculine and feminine substantives have the accusative plural ending in *s*.

TABLE OF THE LATIN DECLENSION.

	Masc. Substantives.		Fem. Substantives.		Neut. Substantives.	
SINGULAR						
N.	us or	[1]	a or	[1]	um or	[1]
G.	i	is.	æ	is.	i	is.
D.	o	i.	æ	i.	o	i.
Ac.	um	em.	am	em.	um	like the nominat.
V.	e	like the nominat.	a	like the nominat	um	like the nominat.
Ab.	o	e.	a	e.	o	i or e.
PLURAL						
N.	i	es.	æ	es.	a	(i)a.
G.	orum	um.	arum	(i)um.	orum	(i)um.
D.	is	ibus.	is	ibus.	is	ibus.
Ac.	os	es.	as	es.	a	(i)a.
V.	i	es.	æ	es.	a	(i)a.
Ab.	is	ibus.	is	ibus.	is	ibus.

FIRST DIVISION.

Declension of Masculine Substantives.

According to their ending in the nominative case, masculine substantives have the genitive in *i* or *is* [1].

I. *I* for all substantives ending in *us.*

II. All others, namely, those that have not their nominative in *us,* have the genitive in *is* added to

---

[1] Substantives having the genitive *is* have a great variety of terminations in the nominative. We give them further on in the declension for each gender, as well as in the General Table for the formation of the genitive in *is.* See end of the declension of nouns.

the root. Nouns of this class have the vocative singular like the nominative, and the nominative, accusative, and vocative plural alike. The change of root in the genitive of these nouns is used for all the other cases. For the formation of the genitive singular, see the general table at the end of the declension of nouns.

EXAMPLES.

I. Of a masculine substantive in *us*.

Singular.		Plural.	
N. Domin*us*,	a lord.	N. Domin*i*,	lords.
G. Domin*i*,	of a lord.	G. Domin*orum*,	of lords.
D. Domin*o*,	to a lord.	D. Domin*is*,	to lords.
A. Domin*um*,	a lord.	A. Domin*os*,	lords.
V. ô Domin*e*,	o lord.	V. ô Domin*i*,	o lords.
A. Domin*o*,	from a lord.	A. Domin*is*,	from lords.

II. Of masculine substantives not having *us* in the nominative, and taking *is* in the genitive.

1. Masculine substantives ending in *o*.

Masculine substantives ending thus have the genitive in *nis*, some adding it simply to the nominative, some changing *o* to *i* short.

a. Substantive masculine in *o*, genitive *onis*.

Singular.		Plural.	
N. Leo,	a lion.	N. Leon*es*,	lions.
G. Leon*is*,	of a lion.	G. Leon*um*,	of lions.
D. Leon*i*,	to a lion.	D. Leon*ibus*,	to lions.
A. Leon*em*,	a lion.	A. Leon*es*,	lions.
V. ô Leo,	o lion.	V. ô Leon*es*,	o lions.
A. Leon*e*,	from a lion.	A. Leon*ibus*,	from lions.

b. Substantive masculine in *o*, genitive *inis*.

Singular.   *Plural.*

N. Hom*o*,	*a man.*	N. Hom*ines*,	*men.*
G. Hom*inis*,	*of a man.*	G. Hom*inum*,	*of men.*
D. Hom*ini*,	*to a man.*	D. Hom*inibus*,	*to men.*
A. Hom*inem*,	*a man.*	A. Hom*ines*,	*men.*
V. ô Hom*o*,	*o man.*	V. ô Hom*ines*,	*o men.*
A. Hom*ine*,	*from a man.*	A. Hom*inibus*,	*from men.*

2. Substantive masculine in *or*, genitive *oris* [2].

N. Error,	*an error.*	N. Error*es*,	*errors.*
G. Error*is*,	*of an error.*	G. Error*um*,	*of errors.*
D. Error*i*,	*to an error.*	D. Error*ibus*,	*to errors.*
A. Error*em*,	*an error.*	A. Error*es*,	*errors.*
V. ô Error,	*o error.*	V. ô Error*es*,	*o errors.*
A. Error*e*,	*from an error.*	A. Error*ibus*,	*from errors.*

3. Substantive masculine ending in *os*, genitive *oris*.

N. Flos,	*a flower.*	N. Flor*es*,	*flowers.*
G. Flor*is*,	*of a flower.*	G. Flor*um*,	*of flowers.*
D. Flor*i*,	*to a flower.*	D. Flor*ibus*,	*to flowers.*
A. Flor*em*,	*a flower.*	A. Flor*es*,	*flowers.*
V. ô Flos,	*o flower.*	V. ô Flor*es*,	*o flowers.*
A. Flor*e*,	*from a flower.*	A. Flor*ibus*,	*from flowers.*

---

[2] Nouns ending in *l, r,* only add to the invariable root the different endings of the cases belonging to the declension which takes *is* in the genitive. Nouns ending in *er* belonging to every declension follow this rule.

4. Substantive masculine in *es*.

To form the genitive, most of these nouns alter *es* into *itis*.

Singular.		*Plural.*	
N. Mil*es*,	*a soldier.*	N. Mil*ites*,	*soldiers.*
G. Mil*itis*,	*of a soldier.*	G. Mil*itum*,	*of soldiers.*
D. Mil*iti*,	*to a soldier.*	D. Mil*itibus*,	*to soldiers.*
A. Mil*item*,	*a soldier.*	A. Mil*ites*,	*soldiers.*
V. ô Mil*es*,	*o soldier.*	V. ô Mil*ites*,	*o soldiers.*
A. Mil*ite*,	*from a soldier.*	A. Mil*itibus*,	*from soldiers.*

5. Substantive masculine in *ex*.

Most of these nouns form the genitive by changing *ex* into *icis*.

Singular.		*Plural.*	
N. Jud*ex*,	*a judge.*	N. Jud*ices*,	*judges.*
G. Jud*icis*,	*of a judge.*	G. Jud*icum*,	*of judges.*
D. Jud*ici*,	*to a judge.*	D. Jud*icibus*,	*to judges.*
A. Jud*icem*,	*a judge.*	A. Jud*ices*,	*judges.*
V. ô Jud*ex*,	*o judge.*	V. ô Jud*ices*,	*o judges.*
A. Jud*ice*,	*from a judge.*	A. Jud*icibus*,	*from judges.*

MASCULINE SUBSTANTIVES.

To serve as examples of the preceding rules.

Amor, *love.*	Aries (*etis*), *a ram.*
Animus, *the soul.*	Asinus, *an ass.*
Apex, *a summit.*	Auctor, *an author.*
Ardor, *ardor.*	Autumnus, *autumn.*

Astronomus, *an astronomer.*
Bacillus, *a wand.*
Baculus, *a stick.*
Bajalus, *a porter.*
Balneator, *a bather.*
Bellator, *a warrior.*
Bufo (*onis*), *a toad.*
Campus, *a field.*
Carbo (*onis*), *coal.*
Caseus, *cheese.*
Cervus, *a stag.*
Cibus, *food.*
Codex, *a code.*
Comes, *a companion.*
Cortex, *bark.*
Custos (*odis*), *a keeper.*
Deceptor, *a deceiver.*
Digitus, *a finger.*
Dolor, *pain.*
Ductor, *a leader.*
Elephantus, *an elephant.*
Emptor, *a purchaser.*
Equus, *a horse.*
Favor, *favor.*
Fluvius, *a river.*
Focus, *a hearth.*
Frutex, *a shrub.*
Fulgor, *brightness.*
Fundus, *the ground.*
Gallus, *a cock.*

Gladius, *a sword.*
Globus, *a globe.*
Grabatus, *a sofa.*
Gubernator, *a governor.*
Gurges, *an abyss.*
Heres (*edis*), *an heir.*
Honor, *honor.*
Horror, *horror.*
Hortus, *a garden.*
Imperator, *an emperor.*
Index, *an informer.*
Inventor, *an inventor.*
Jocus, *a joke.*
Labor, *work.*
Lac (gen. *lactis*), *milk.*
Latro (*onis*), *a robber.*
Lectus, *a bed.*
Legatus, *an ambassador.*
Lepor, *mirth.*
Locus, *a place.*
Lupus, *a wolf.*
Medicus, *a doctor.*
Mercator, *a merchant.*
Modus, *a method.*
Mos, *a custom.*
Nebulo (*onis*), *a rascal.*
Nemo (*inis*), *nobody* [a].
Nidus, *a nest.*
Nitor, *splendor.*
Numerus, *a number.*

---

[a] Has no plural.

Nuntius, *a messenger.*
Oceanus, *the ocean.*
Oculus, *the eye.*
Odor, *a smell.*
Opifex, *a workman.*
Orator, *an orator.*
Pavo (*onis*), *a peacock.*
Pavor, *fear.*
Pedes, *a foot soldier.*
Pedisequus, *a footman.*
Pes (*edis*), *the foot.*
Pictor, *a painter.*
Piscator, *a fisherman.*
Pollex, *the thumb.*
Pontifex, *a pontiff.*
Populus, *the people.*
Porcus, *a hog.*
Præceptor, *a tutor.*
Præco (*onis*), *a herald.*
Prætor, *a prætor.*
Proditor, *a traitor.*
Pudor, *modesty.*
Pullus, *a chicken.*
Quæstor, *a quæstor.*
Radius, *a ray.*
Ramus, *a bough.*
Rector, *a governor.*

Rex (*egis*), *a king.*
Rivus, *a river.*
Ros, *dew.*
Rumor, *rumour.*
Sacerdos (*otis*), *priest.*
Satelles, *a satellite.*
Sermo (*onis*), *a speech.*
Servus, *a slave.*
Silex, *a pebble.*
Socius, *a companion.*
Somnus, *sleep.*
Sutor, *a shoemaker.*
Scriptor, *a writer.*
Taurus, *a bull.*
Terror, *terror.*
Timor, *fear.*
Tiro, *a recruit.*
Tonsor, *a barber.*
Turbo (*inis*), *a whirlwind.*
Tutor, *a tutor.*
Ursus, *a bear.*
Vapor, *vapour.*
Ventus, *the wind.*
Vertex, *a summit.*
Viator, *a traveller.*
Victor, *a victor.*
Vitulus, *a calf.*

EXCEPTION I.

A certain number of substantives having the nominative singular in *er* (formerly *erus*) drop the syllable *us*. These nouns are declined exactly like

B

those in *us*, with this difference, that they do not take *e* in the vocative. They mostly drop the letter *e* of the root.

EXAMPLE

1. Of a masculine substantive in *er*, genitive *i*, dropping the letter *e* of the root.

Singular.   *Plural.*

N. Lib*er*,	*a book.*	N. Lib*ri*,	*books.*
G. Lib*ri*,	*of a book.*	G. Lib*rorum*,	*of books.*
D. Lib*ro*,	*to a book.*	D. Lib*ris*,	*to books.*
A. Lib*rum*,	*a book.*	A. Lib*ros*,	*books.*
V. ô Lib*er*,	*o book.*	V. ô Lib*ri*,	*o books.*
A. Lib*ro*,	*from a book.*	A. Lib*ris*,	*from books.*

Decline in the same manner :

Ager, *a field.*	Coluber, *a snake.*
Aper, *a boar.*	Faber, *a workman.*
Arbiter, *an arbitrator.*	Magister, *a master.*
Auster, *the south wind.*	Minister, *a minister.*
Cancer, *a crab.*	

2. Of a masculine substantive in *er*, retaining the letter *e* of the root.

N. Puer,	*a boy.*	N. Pue*ri*,	*boys.*
G. Pue*ri*,	*of a boy.*	G. Pue*rorum*,	*of boys.*
D. Pue*ro*,	*to a boy.*	D. Pue*ris*,	*to boys.*
A. Pue*rum*,	*a boy.*	A. Pue*ros*,	*boys.*
V. ô Puer,	*o boy.*	V. ô Pue*ri*,	*o boys.*
A. Pue*ro*,	*from a boy.*	A. Pue*ris*,	*from boys.*

Decline in the same manner:

Adulter, *an adulterer.*	Lucifer, *the morning star.*
Gener, *a son-in-law.*	Socer, *a father-in-law.*
Laniger, *a sheep.*	Vesper, *evening.*

Exception II.

There are also some masculine substantives in *er* that have the genitive in *is,* some rejecting the *e,* others retaining it. All those ending in *ter* and *ber* drop it. For example: *pater,* a father, *patris; imber,* rain, *imbris;* with the exception of *later,* a brick, which becomes *lateris.* The others retain the *e:* *passer,* a sparrow, *passeris.*

Example

Of a masculine substantive in *er,* genitive *is* [4].

Singular.		*Plural.*	
N. Anser,	*a goose.*	N. Anseres,	*geese.*
G. Anseris,	*of a goose.*	G. Anserum,	*of geese.*
D. Anseri,	*to a goose.*	D. Anseribus,	*to geese.*
A. Anserem,	*a goose.*	A. Anseres,	*geese.*
V. ô Anser,	*o goose.*	V. ô Anseres,	*o geese.*
A. Ansere,	*from a goose.*	A. Anseribus,	*from geese.*

The following are declined thus, retaining the *e:*

Aer, *air.*	Later, *a brick.*
Æther, *ether.*	Passer, *a sparrow.*
Agger, *a heap.*	Vomer, *a ploughshare.*
Carcer, *a prison.*	

[4] See note 2, p. 10.

These reject the *e* :

Accipiter, *a hawk.*	Pater, *a father.*
Frater, *a brother.*	Venter, *the stomach.*
Imber, *a shower.*	

OBSERVATIONS.

Obs. A. One noun only of this declension has the nominative case ending in *ir*, viz. *vir*, a man. However *vir* and its compounds, as *levir*, a brother-in-law, *duumvir, triumvir, decemvir, centumvir*, are declined exactly like *puer*.

Obs. B. Proper names ending in *ius* and *jus* have the vocative in *i* instead of *e;* ex. : *Horatius*, Horace, voc. *Horati; Pompejus*, Pompey, voc. *Pompei*. Common nouns, having the same ending, are declined in the same manner : *filius*, a son, and *genius*, a genius, which have *fili* and *geni* in the vocative [5].

Decline the following examples : *Gajus, Mercurius*, Mercury ; *Virgilius*, Virgil ; *Terentius*, Terence ; *Spurius, Cassius, Manlius, Tullius* [6].

Obs. C. Deus, God, has its vocative *Deus*, the nominative and vocative plural, *Dii* or *Di*, and the dative plural, *Diis* or *Dis*.

Obs. D. Several nouns ending in *us* have the genitive plural in *ûm* instead of *orum*. They are as follows :—

[5] Proper names, originally adjectives, like nouns ending in *ius*, being derived from the Greek, have the vocative in *ie;* ex. *Darius*, vocative *Darie; Pius*, vocative *Pie*.

[6] Many Latin proper names retain their ending in English.

1. The names of coins and measures:

	Genitive plural.
Denarius, *a penny.*	Denariûm.
Modius, *a bushel.*	Modiûm.
Nummus, *a coin.*	Nummûm.
Sestertius, *a sesterce.*	Sestertiûm.

2. Some names of nations, in poetry, but rarely in prose, as *Argivûm, Danaûm, Pelasgûm,* instead of *Argivorum, Danaorum, Pelasgorum,* &c.

3. The following nouns:

	Genitive plural.
Deus, *God.*	Deûm.
Faber, *an artisan.*	Fabrûm.
Liber, *a child.*	Liberûm.
Procus, *a suitor.*	Procûm.

And the compounds of *vir,* a man, *duumvir, triumvir, decemvir.*

EXCEPTION III.

A certain number of masculine substantives, ending mostly in *sus* and *tus,* are declined in the following manner :—

Singular.		*Plural.*	
N. Fruct*us,*	*fruit.*	N. Fruct*us,*	*fruits.*
G. Fruct*ûs,*	*of fruit.*	G. Fruct*uum,*	*of fruits.*
D. Fruct*ui,*	*to fruit.*	D. Fruct*ibus,*	*to fruits.*
A. Fruct*um,*	*fruit.*	A. Fruct*us,*	*fruits.*
V. Fruct*us,*	*o fruit.*	V. Fruct*us,*	*o fruits.*
A. Fruct*u,*	*from fruit.*	A. Fruct*ibus,*	*from fruits.*

Those most generally in use are:

Accentus, *an accent.*
Actus, *an act.*
Adventus, *an arrival.*
Æstus, *heat.*
Appetitus, *an appetite.*
Arcus, *a bow* (dat. pl. *ubus*).
Aspectus, *an aspect.*
Cantus, *a song.*
Cœtus, *an assembly.*
Casus, *a case.*
Consulatus, *the consulate.*
Effectus, *an effect.*
Equitatus, *equitation.*
Exercitus, *an army.*
Exitus, *an exit.*
Gestus, *a gesture.*
Gradus, *a degree.*
Habitus, *a habit.*
Lacus, *a lake* (dat. pl. *ubus*).
Lapsus, *a fall.*

Lusus, *a game.*
Magistratus, *a magistrate.*
Morsus, *a bite.*
Motus, *a motion.*
Passus, *a step.*
Portus, *a harbour* (dat. pl. *ubus*).
Risus, *laughter.*
Senatus, *a senate.*
Sensus, *sense.*
Sinus, *the bosom* (dat. pl. *ubus*).
Specus, *a den* (dat. pl. *ubus*).
Status, *state.*
Sumptus, *expense.*
Tactus, *a touch.*
Tribunatus, *the tribunate.*
Tumultus, *a tumult.*
Usus, *use.*
Visus, *the sight.*
Vultus, *the countenance.*

Obs. A. The dative singular of these nouns ends often in *u* instead of *ui*. Ex.: *senatus*, dat. *senatu.*

Obs. B. The noun *domus*, house, is declined in some cases like nouns in *us*, genitive *i*; in others like the above nouns [7].

[7] The following verse shows the terminations that are foreign to this word:—

> Tolle *me, mu, mi, mis,* si declinare *domus* vis.
> Take away *me, mu, mi, mis,* if you will decline *domus.*

Singular.		Plural.	
N. Dom*us*,	a house.	N. Dom*us*,	houses.
G. Dom*us*,	of a house.	G. Dom*uum*, or dom*orum*,	
			of houses.
D. Dom*ui*,	to a house.	D. Dom*ibus*,	to houses.
A. Dom*um*,	a house.	A. Dom*os*,	houses.
V. Dom*us*,	o house.	V. Dom*us*,	o houses.
A. Dom*o*,	from a house.	A. Dom*ibus*,	from houses.

SECOND DIVISION.

Declension of Feminine Substantives.

Feminine substantives have the genitive in *æ* or in *is*, according to the termination of the nominative.

I. All those ending in *a* in the nominative have the genitive in *æ*.

II. All the others, (namely, those which do not end in *a* for the nominative) have the genitive in *is*, adding this ending to the root. The vocative singular is like the nominative, and in the plural, the nominative, accusative, and vocative are all three alike. The change in the root for the genitive singular is continued through the other cases. The declension is the same as that of the masculine nouns having the genitive in *is*. (See the General Table at the end of the declension of the nouns.)

EXAMPLES.

I. Of a feminine substantive in *a*.

Singular.		*Plural.*	
N. Mensa,	*a table.*	N. Mensæ,	*tables.*
G. Mensæ,	*of a table.*	G. Mensarum,	*of tables.*
D. Mensæ,	*to a table.*	D. Mensis,	*to tables.*
A. Mensam,	*a table.*	A. Mensas,	*tables.*
V. ô Mensa,	*o table.*	V. ô Mensæ,	*o tables.*
A. Mensa,	*from a table.*	A. Mensis,	*from tables.*

Obs. Asina, a she-ass, *filia,* a daughter, have the dative and ablative plural *asinabus, filiabus,* to distinguish them from the masculine *asinus, filius,* which alter to *asinis, filiis.* Also *dea,* a goddess, has the dative and ablative plural *deabus.*

II. Feminine substantives not ending in *a* in the nominative, and having *is* in the genitive.

1. Feminine substantives in *io.* This termination retains the *o.*

Singular.		*Plural.*	
N. Ratio,	*reason.*	N. Rationes,	*reasons.*
G. Rationis,	*of reason.*	G. Rationum,	*of reasons.*
D. Rationi,	*to reason.*	D. Rationibus,	*to reasons.*
A. Rationem,	*reason.*	A. Rationes,	*reasons.*
V. ô Ratio,	*o reason.*	V. ô Rationes,	*o reasons.*
A. Ratione,	*from reason.*	A. Rationibus,	*from reasons.*

2. Substantive feminine ending in *go*. This termination changes *o* into *i* short.

Singular.		Plural.	
N. Ori*go*,	*origin.*	N. Ori*gines*,	*origins.*
G. Ori*ginis*,	*of origin.*	G. Ori*ginum*,	*of origins.*
D. Ori*gini*,	*to origin.*	D. Ori*ginibus*,	*to origins.*
A. Ori*ginem*,	*origin.*	A. Ori*gines*,	*origins.*
V. ô Ori*go*,	*o origin.*	V. ô Ori*gines*,	*o origins.*
A. Ori*gine*,	*from origin.*	A. Ori*ginibus*,	*from origins.*

3. Substantive feminine ending in *do*. This termination changes *o* into *i* short.

Singular.		Plural.	
N. Consuetu*do*,	*custom.*	N. Consuetu*dines*,	*customs.*
G. Consuetu*dinis*,	*of custom.*	G. Consuetu*dinum*,	*of customs.*
D. Consuetu*dini*,	*to custom.*	D. Consuetu*dinibus*,	*to customs.*
A. Consuetu*dinem*,	*custom.*	A. Consuetu*dines*,	*customs.*
V. ô Consuetu*do*,	*o custom.*	V. ô Consuetu*dines*,	*o customs.*
A. Consuetu*dine*,	*from custom.*	A. Consuetu*dinibus*,	*from customs.*

4. Substantive feminine in *as*.

Singular.		Plural.	
N. Æt*as*,	*an age.*	N. Æt*ates*,	*ages.*
G. Æta*tis*,	*of an age.*	G. Æta*tum*,	*of ages.*
D. Æta*ti*,	*to an age.*	D. Æta*tibus*,	*to ages.*
A. Æta*tem*,	*an age.*	A. Æt*ates*,	*ages.*
V. ô Æt*as*,	*o age.*	V. ô Æt*ates*,	*o ages.*
A. Æta*te*,	*from an age.*	A. Æta*tibus*,	*from ages.*

5. Substantive feminine in *x*. These nouns alter *x* to *cis*.

Singular.		Plural.	
N. Fa*x*,	a torch.	N. Fa*ces*,	torches.
G. Fa*cis*,	of a torch.	G. Fa*cum*,	of torches.
D. Fa*ci*,	to a torch.	D. Fa*cibus*,	to torches.
A. Fa*cem*,	a torch.	A. Fa*ces*,	torches.
V. ô Fa*x*,	o torch.	V. ô Fa*ces*,	o torches.
A. Fa*ce*,	from a torch.	A. Fa*cibus*,	from torches.

6. Substantive feminine in *is*.

N. Aur*is*,	an ear.	N. Aur*es*,	ears.
G. Aur*is*,	of an ear.	G. Aur*ium*,	of ears.
D. Aur*i*,	to an ear.	D. Aur*ibus*,	to ears.
A. Aur*em*,	an ear.	A. Aur*es*,	ears.
V. ô Aur*is*,	o ear.	V. ô Aur*es*,	o ears.
A. Aur*e*,	from an ear.	A. Aur*ibus*,	from ears.

7. Substantive feminine in *es*.

N. Nub*es*,	a cloud.	N. Nub*es*,	clouds.
G. Nub*is*,	of a cloud.	G. Nub*ium*,	of clouds.
D. Nub*i*,	to a cloud.	D. Nub*ibus*,	to clouds.
A. Nub*em*,	a cloud.	A. Nub*es*,	clouds.
V. ô Nub*es*,	o cloud.	V. ô Nub*es*,	o clouds.
A. Nub*e*,	from a cloud.	A. Nub*ibus*,	from clouds.

8. Substantive feminine in *s* preceded by a consonant.

N. Ar*s*,	an art.	N. Ar*tes*,	arts.
G. Ar*tis*,	of an art.	G. Ar*tium*,	of arts.
D. Ar*ti*,	to an art.	D. Ar*tibus*,	to arts.
A. Ar*tem*,	an art.	A. Ar*tes*,	arts.
V. ô Ar*s*,	o art.	V. ô Ar*tes*,	o arts.
A. Ar*te*,	from an art.	A. Ar*tibus*,	from arts.

Obs. Most substantives having the last three endings, *is, es, rs,* have *ium* in the genitive plural.

FEMININE SUBSTANTIVES.

To serve as examples to the preceding rules.

Abundantia, *abundance.*

Ala, *a wing.*

Alauda, *a lark.*

Amicitia, *friendship.*

Anguis, *a serpent.*

Ancilla, *a maidservant.*

Anima, *the soul.*

Apis, *a bee.*

Aqua, *water.*

Aquila, *an eagle.*

Ara, *an altar.*

Arena, *sand.*

Arx, *a castle.*

Avis, *a bird.*

Balæna, *a whale.*

Barba, *the beard.*

Bellua, *a beast.*

Bacca, *a berry.*

Benevolentia, *benevolence.*

Bibliotheca, *a library.*

Brevitas, *brevity.*

Cædes, *slaughter.*

Calamitas, *calamity.*

Calx, *the heel.*

Caro (gen. *carnis*), *flesh.*

Causa, *a cause.*

Cerevisia, *beer.*

Charta, *paper.*

Civitas, *a state.*

Claritas, *clearness.*

Columba, *a dove.*

Commendatio (*onis*), *a recommendation.*

Conscientia, *conscience.*

Consolatio (*onis*), *consolation.*

Cupiditas, *covetousness.*

Custodia, *a guard.*

Deditio (*onis*), *surrender.*

Deformitas, *deformity.*

Dignitas, *dignity.*

Dilatio (*onis*), *delay.*

Diligentia, *care.*

Disciplina, *tuition.*

Discordia, *discord.*

Ditio (*onis*), *dominion.*

Doctrina, *doctrine.*

Dominatrix, *a ruler.*

Ebrietas, *intoxication.*

Educatio (*onis*), *education.*
Egestas, *poverty.*
Eloquentia, *eloquence.*
Emendatio (*onis*), *correction.*
Epistola, *a letter.*
Equa, *a mare.*
Eruca, *a caterpillar.*
Esca, *food.*
Exceptio (*onis*), *an exception.*
Exercitatio (*onis*), *exercise.*
Experientia, *experience.*
Exspectatio (*onis*), *expectation.*
Fabula, *a fable.*
Facultas, *power.*
Falx, *a scythe.*
Fama, *fame.*
Fames, *hunger.*
Familia, *a family.*
Familiaritas, *familiarity.*
Fax, *a torch.*
Felicitas, *happiness.*
Felis, *a cat.*
Fenestra, *a window.*
Forma, *a form.*
Formica, *an ant.*
Formido (*inis*), *fear.*
Fornax, *an oven.*
Fraus (gen. *fraudis*), *fraud.*
Gallina, *a hen.*

Garrulitas, *gossip.*
Gemma, *a gem.*
Gens, *a race.*
Glans (gen. *glandis*), *an acorn.*
Gleba, *a clod.*
Gloria, *glory.*
Grando (*inis*), *hail.*
Gratulatio (*onis*), *congratulation.*
Gravitas, *gravity.*
Hasta, *a lance.*
Herba, *an herb.*
Hiems (gen. *hiemis*), *winter.*
Hilaritas, *hilarity.*
Historia, *a history.*
Honestas, *honesty.*
Hora, *an hour.*
Ignavia, *cowardice.*
Ignominia, *ignominy.*
Immanitas, *cruelty.*
Immortalitas, *immortality.*
Impietas, *impiety.*
Improbitas, *dishonesty.*
Indagatio (*onis*), *investigation.*
Insula, *an island.*
Invidia, *envy.*
Janua, *a door.*
Lanx, *a scale.*
Lacryma, *a tear.*

Legio (*onis*), *a legion.*
Levitas, *levity.*
Libertas, *liberty.*
Libido (*inis*), *covetousness.*
Lingua, *the tongue.*
Littera, *a letter of the alphabet.*
Luna, *the moon.*
Luscinia, *a nightingale.*
Lux, *light.*
Luxuria, *luxury.*
Machina, *a machine.*
Magnitudo (*inis*), *greatness.*
Mens, *the mind.*
Mensa, *a table.*
Mentio (*onis*), *mention.*
Merx, *merchandise.*
Mora, *delay.*
Multitudo (*inis*), *a multitude.*
Mutatio (*onis*), *an alteration.*
Naris, *the nostril.*
Natio (*onis*), *a nation.*
Natura, *nature.*
Necessitudo (*inis*), *necessity.*
Nix (gen. *nivis*), *snow.*
Noverca, *a mother-in-law.*
Nox (gen. *noctis*), *night.*
Noxa, *an injury.*

Oblivio (*onis*), *forgetfulness.*
Obsidio (*onis*), *a siege.*
Occasio (*onis*), *an opportunity.*
Offensa, *an annoyance.*
Opera, *a work.*
Ops (gen. *opis*), *assistance.*
Oratio (*onis*), *a speech.*
Ovis, *a sheep.*
Patria, *one's native country.*
Paupertas, *poverty.*
Pecunia, *money.*
Pellis, *the skin.*
Penna, *a feather.*
Perspicuitas, *sagacity.*
Pestis, *the plague.*
Pietas, *piety.*
Pigritia, *slothfulness.*
Plaga, *a blow.*
Plebs (gen. *plebis*), *the people.*
Pluma, *a feather.*
Pluvia, *rain.*
Pœna, *a penalty.*
Popina, *a kitchen.*
Possessio (*onis*), *possession.*
Potio (*onis*), *drink.*
Præda, *a prey.*
Quæstura, *the quæstorship.*

c

Radix, *a root.*
Rana, *a frog.*
Regina, *a queen.*
Regio (*onis*), *a region.*
Regula, *a rule.*
Religio (*onis*), *religion.*
Responsio (*onis*), *an answer.*
Ripa, *the shore.*
Rixa, *a quarrel.*
Ruga, *a wrinkle.*
Sagitta, *an arrow.*
Sapientia, *wisdom.*
Schola, *a school.*
Securitas, *safety.*
Sedes, *a seat.*
Sepes, *a hedge.*
Serpens, *a serpent.*
Silva, *a forest.*
Societas, *society.*
Solitudo (*inis*), *solitude.*
Sollicitudo (*inis*), *solicitude.*
Sors, *fate.*
Sphæra, *a globe.*
Stella, *a star.*
Stirps (gen. *stirpis*), *the trunk* (of a tree).

Strages, *a defeat.*
Superstitio (*onis*), *superstition.*
Tabella, *a tablet.*
Talpa, *a mole.*
Temeritas, *rashness.*
Tempestas, *a tempest.*
Terra, *the earth.*
Trabs (gen. *trabis*), *a beam.*
Tutela, *a protection.*
Umbra, *a shadow.*
Unda, *a wave.*
Urbs (gen. *urbis*), *a city.*
Utilitas, *usefulness.*
Uva, *a grape.*
Valetudo (*inis*), *health.*
Veritas, *truth.*
Vestis, *a garment.*
Via, *a road.*
Victoria, *victory.*
Virgo (*inis*), *a virgin.*
Vita, *life.*
Vitis, *a vine.*
Voluntas, *the will.*
Vorago (*inis*), *an abyss.*
Vox, *the voice.*

EXCEPTION I.

A certain number of feminine substantives in *ies* (seldom in *es*) are declined in the following manner :-

Singular.		*Plural.*	
N. Species,	*a form.*	N. Species,	*forms.*
G. Speciei,	*of a form.*	G. Specierum,	*of forms.*
D. Speciei,	*to a form.*	D. Speciebus,	*to forms.*
A. Speciem,	*a form.*	A. Species,	*forms.*
V. ô Species,	*o form.*	V. Species,	*o forms.*
A. Specie,	*from a form.*	A. Speciebus,	*from forms.*

Decline thus :

Acies, *a fight.*	Mollities, *softness.*
Barbaries, *barbarism.*	Pernicies, *ruin.*
Blandities, *flattery.*	Pigrities, *idleness.*
Calvities, *baldness.*	Planities, *a plain.*
Durities, *hardness.*	Progenies, *a race.*
Effigies, *an effigy.*	Rabies, *rage.*
Facies, *the face.*	Res, *a thing.*
Fides, *faith.*	Segnities, *laziness.*
Glacies, *ice.*	Series, *a series.*
Luxuries, *lasciviousness.*	Species, *a form.*
Materies, *matter.*	Spes, *hope.*

Obs. A. Dies, day, and *meridies*, noon, which are declined in the same way, are masculine. See further on for the rules on gender.

Obs. B. Most of these, being abstract nouns, admit of no plural. *Res, species*, and the masculine *dies*, are the only ones that have all the plural cases ; *acies, facies, effigies, series, spes*, only have the nominative and accusative plural.

EXCEPTION II.

There are also feminine substantives in *us;* some have the genitive, like the masculine nouns, ending in *i*; others have the genitive in *ûs*.like the masculine (Exception III. p. 17) ; lastly, others have the genitive in *utis* and *udis*.   (See the rules on gender.)

1. Feminine substantive in *us*, genitive *i*.

Singular.		*Plural.*	
N. Aln*us*,	*an alder.*	N. Aln*i*,	*alders.*
G. Aln*i*,	*of an alder.*	G. Aln*orum*,	*of alders.*
D. Aln*o*,	*to an alder.*	D. Aln*is*,	*to alders.*
A. Aln*um*,	*an alder.*	A. Aln*os*,	*alders.*
V. ô Aln*e*,	*o alder.*	V. ô Aln*i*,	*o alders.*
A. Aln*o*,	*from an alder.*	A. Aln*is*,	*from alders.*

Decline thus :

Alvus, *the belly.*	Humus, *the ground.*
Arctus, *the bear (constella-*	Malus, *an apple-tree.*
tion).	Prunus, *a plum-tree.*
Cerasus, *a cherry-tree.*	Vannus, *a fan.*
Colus, *a distaff.*	

2. Feminine substantive in *us*, genitive *ûs*.

Singular.		*Plural.*	
N. Man*us*,	*the hand.*	N. Man*us*,	*the hands.*
G. Man*ûs*,	*of the hand.*	G. Man*uum*,	*of the hands.*
D. Man*ui*,	*to the hand.*	D. Man*ibus*,	*to the hands.*
A. Man*um*,	*the hand.*	A. Man*us*,	*the hands.*
V. ô Man*us*,	*o hand.*	V. ô Man*us*,	*o hands.*
A. Man*u*,	*from the hand.*	A. Man*ibus*,	*from the hands.*

Decline in the same manner,

Acus, *a needle.*	Ficus, *a fig-tree.*
Anus, *an old woman.*	Nurus, *a daughter-in-law.*

Porticus, *a portico.*

Quercus, *an oak.* (dat. pl. ubus).

Socrus, *a mother-in-law.*

Tribus, *a tribe* (dat. pl. ubus).

3. Substantive feminine in *us*, genitive *utis.*

Singular.		*Plural.*	
N. Virtus,	*virtue.*	N. Virtutes,	*virtues.*
G. Virtutis,	*of virtue.*	G. Virtutum,	*of virtues.*
D. Virtuti,	*to virtue.*	D. Virtutibus,	*to virtues.*
A. Virtutem,	*virtue.*	A. Virtutes,	*virtues.*
V. ô Virtus,	*o virtue.*	V. ô Virtutes,	*o virtues.*
A. Virtute,	*from virtue.*	A. Virtutibus,	*from virtues.*

Decline in the same manner,

Juventus, *youth.*

Salus, *safety.*

Senectus, *old age.*

Servitus, *servitude.*

4. Substantive feminine in *us*, genitive *udis.*

Singular.		*Plural.*	
N. Incus,	*an anvil.*	N. Incudes,	*anvils.*
G. Incudis,	*of an anvil.*	G. Incudum,	*of anvils.*
D. Incudi,	*to an anvil.*	D. Incudibus,	*to anvils.*
A. Incudem,	*an anvil.*	A. Incudes,	*anvils.*
V. ô Incus,	*o anvil.*	V. ô Incudes,	*o anvils.*
A. Incude,	*from an anvil.*	A. Incudibus,	*from anvils.*

Decline in the same manner,

Palus, *a marsh.*

Pecus, *cattle.*

Subscus, *a joiner's dovetail.*

EXCEPTION III.

There are also feminine substantives in *er*, genitive *is*, that have the same peculiarities as the masculine (Exception II. p. 15), by suppressing the *e;* as in *mater,* mother, genitive *matris.*

Substantive feminine in *er,* genitive *is.*

Singular.		*Plural.*	
N. Mulier,	*a woman.*	N. Mulieres,	*women.*
G. Mulieris,	*of a woman.*	G. Mulierum,	*of women.*
D. Mulieri,	*to a woman.*	D. Mulieribus,	*to women.*
A. Mulierem,	*a woman.*	A. Mulieres,	*women.*
V. ô Mulier,	*o woman.*	V. ô Mulieres,	*o women.*
A. Muliere,	*from a woman.*	A. Mulieribus,	*from women.*

Decline in the same manner,

Linter, *a boat.* | Tuber, *a tuber-tree.*

THIRD DIVISION.

Declension of Neuter Substantives.

A. All neuter substantives have three cases alike in the singular and plural: the *Nominative, Accusative,* and *Vocative.* (See Preliminary Remark C, p. 7.)

B. According to their ending in the nominative, neuter substantives have the genitive case in *i* or *is.*

I. All those which have the nominative case ending in *um,* have the genitive in *i.*

II. All the others, namely, those which do not end in *um,* have the genitive in *is,* added to the root. (See the general Table at the end of the Declension of Nouns.).

EXAMPLES.

I. Of a neuter substantive in *um*.

Singular.		*Plural.*	
N. Bell*um*,	*war.*	N. Bell*a*,	*wars.*
G. Bell*i*,	*of war.*	G. Bell*orum*,	*of wars.*
D. Bell*o*,	*to war.*	D. Bell*is*,	*to wars.*
A. Bell*um*,	*war.*	A. Bell*a*,	*wars.*
V. ô Bell*um*,	*o war.*	V. ô Bell*a*,	*o wars.*
A. Bell*o*,	*from war.*	A. Bell*is*,	*from wars.*

II. Of neuter substantives not ending in *um* in the nominative, and having *is* in the genitive.

The neuter nouns ending in *e*, *al*, *ar*, genitive *is*, have the ablative singular in *i*, the nominative plural in *ia*, and the genitive plural in *ium*.

1. Neuter substantive in *e*.

Singular.		*Plural.*	
N. Mar*e*,	*the sea.*	N. Mar*ia*,	*seas.*
G. Mar*is*,	*of the sea.*	G. Mar*ium*,	*of seas.*
D. Mar*i*,	*to the sea.*	D. Mar*ibus*,	*to seas.*
A. Mar*e*,	*the sea.*	A. Mar*ia*,	*seas.*
V. ô Mar*e*,	*o sea.*	V. ô Mar*ia*,	*o seas.*
A. Mar*i*,	*from the sea.*	A. Mar*ibus*,	*from seas.*

2. Neuter substantive in *al*[a].

N. Animal,	*an animal.*	N. Animal*ia*,	*animals.*
G. Animal*is*,	*of an animal.*	G. Animal*ium*,	*of animals.*
D. Animal*i*,	*to an animal.*	D. Animal*ibus*,	*to animals.*

[a] See note 2, p. 10.

Singular.		*Plural.*	
A. Animal,	an animal.	A. Animalia,	animals.
V. ô Animal,	o animal.	V. ô Animalia,	o animals.
A. Animali,	from an animal.	A. Animalibus,	from animals.

3. Neuter substantive in *ar*.

N. Calcar,	a spur.	N. Calcaria,	spurs.
G. Calcaris,	of a spur.	G. Calcarium,	of spurs.
D. Calcari,	to a spur.	D. Calcaribus,	to spurs.
A. Calcar,	a spur.	A. Calcaria,	spurs.
V. ô Calcar,	o spur.	V. ô Calcaria,	o spurs.
A. Calcari,	from a spur.	A. Calcaribus,	from spurs.

4. Neuter substantive in *ur*.

N. Fulgur,	a thunderbolt.	N. Fulgura,	thunderbolts.
G. Fulguris,	of a thunderbolt.	G. Fulgurum,	of thunderbolts.
D. Fulguri,	to a thunderbolt.	D. Fulguribus,	to thunderbolts.
A. Fulgur,	a thunderbolt.	A. Fulgura,	thunderbolts.
V. ô Fulgur,	o thunderbolt.	V. ô Fulgura,	o thunderbolts.
A. Fulgure,	from a thunderbolt.	A. Fulguribus,	from thunderbolts.

Obs. Several neuter substantives in *ur* change the *u* of the root into *o* in the genitive, and in all the cases that end differently from the nominative singular. Ex. *femur,* the thigh ; *femoris,.femori, femore, femora, femorum, femoribus.* (See p. 51.)

5. Substantive neuter in *en,* changing *en* into *inis.*

Singular.		*Plural.*	
N. Flum*en,*	*a river.*	N. Flum*ina,*	*rivers.*
G. Flum*inis,*	*of a river.*	G. Flum*inum,*	*of rivers.*
D. Flum*ini,*	*to a river.*	D. Flum*inibus,*	*to rivers.*
A. Flum*en,*	*a river.*	A. Flum*ina,*	*rivers.*
V. ô Flum*en,*	*o river.*	V. ô Flum*ina,*	*o rivers.*
A. Flum*ine, from a river.*		A. Flum*inibus,*	*from rivers.*

NEUTER SUBSTANTIVES.

To serve as examples to the preceding rules.

Ærarium, *a treasury.*
Agmen, *a troop.*
Alimentum, *food.*
Altare, *an altar.*
Aratrum, *a plough.*
Argentum, *silver.*
Arvum, *a meadow.*
Atramentum, *ink.*
Aulæum, *a curtain.*
Auxilium, *aid.*
Beneficium, *a benefit.*
Bonum, *a benefit.*
Bovile, *an ox stall.*
Caput (*itis*), *the head.*

Carmen, *a song.*
Cervical, *a pillow.*
Cochlear, *a spoon.*
Cognomen, *a surname.*
Collum, *the neck.*
Commodum, *an advantage.*
Conclave, *an apartment.*
Consilium, *deliberation.*
Crimen, *a crime.*
Cubile, *a bed.*
Culmen, *the summit.*
Damnum, *damage.*
Desiderium, *a wish.*
Discrimen, *danger.*

Dolium, *a cask.*
Donum, *a gift.*
Ebur (*oris*), *ivory.*
Emolumentum, *an advantage.*
Examen, *an examination.*
Exemplar, *a pattern.*
Exemplum, *an example.*
Exitium, *loss.*
Exsilium, *exile.*
Factum, *a fact.*
Femur (*oris*), *the hip.*
Flumen, *a river.*
Forum, *a public place.*
Frumentum, *wheat.*
Fundamentum, *a foundation.*
Gaudium, *joy.*
Gramen, *grass.*
Gremium, *the bosom.*
Gubernaculum, *the helm.*
Guttur, *the throat.*
Hastile, *a spear.*
Homicidium, *murder.*
Horologium, *a watch.*
Horreum, *a barn.*
Imperium, *a reign.*
Initium, *the beginning.*
Jecur (*oris*), *the liver.*
Jubar, *splendour.*
Judicium, *judgment.*
Jugum, *a yoke.*

Latibulum, *a hiding place.*
Lignum, *wood.*
Lilium, *a lily.*
Limen, *the threshold.*
Lumen, *light.*
Malum, *evil.*
Matrimonium, *marriage.*
Membrum, *a limb.*
Monile, *a necklace.*
Murmur, *a murmur.*
Navigium, *a ship.*
Nectar, *nectar.*
Negotium, *business.*
Nomen, *a name.*
Nubilum, *a cloud.*
Odium, *hatred.*
Officium, *duty.*
Oppidum, *a town.*
Oraculum, *an oracle.*
Ornamentum, *an ornament.*
Otium, *leisure.*
Ovile, *a sheepfold.*
Ovum, *an egg.*
Pecten, *a comb.*
Periculum, *danger.*
Pilum, *a javelin.*
Poculum, *a cup.*
Præmium, *a reward.*
Præsepe, *a manger.*
Probrum, *shame.*

Prælium, *a battle.*
Pulvinar, *a cushion.*
Regnum, *a reign.*
Remedium, *a remedy.*
Responsum, *an answer.*
Rete, *a snare.*
Robur (*oris*), *heart of oak.*
Rostrum, *a beak.*
Scamnum, *a bench.*
Sepulcrum, *a sepulchre.*
Signum, *a sign.*
Solamen, *consolation.*
Solatium, *solace.*
Spatium, *space.*
Studium, *study.*

Sulfur, *sulphur.*
Supplicium, *an atonement.*
Templum, *a temple.*
Tentamen, *a trial.*
Tergum, *the back.*
Testimonium, *testimony.*
Tribunal, *a tribunal.*
Umbraculum, *shade.*
Unguentum, *ointment.*
Vectigal, *a toll.*
Verbum, *a word.*
Vinculum, *a bond* (*tie*).
Vinum, *wine.*
Vitium, *vice.*

Exception I.

A certain number of neuter substantives end in *u ;* they are invariable in the singular, and in the plural follow the declension of masculine nouns in *us*, genitive *ûs* [*]. (See p. 17.)

Singular.		*Plural.*	
N. Cornu,	*a horn.*	N. Cornu*a*,	*horns.*
G. Cornu,	*of a horn.*	G. Cornu*um*,	*of horns.*
D. Cornu,	*to a horn.*	D. Corni*bus*,	*to horns.*
A. Cornu,	*a horn.*	A. Cornu*a*,	*horns.*
V. ô Cornu,	*o horn.*	V. ô Cornu*a*,	*o horns.*
A. Cornu,	*from a horn.*	A. Corni*bus*,	*from horns.*

[*] Except the three cases that are alike.

Decline in the same manner,

Genu, *the knee.*	Tonitru, *thunder.*
Pecu, *cattle.*	Veru, *a spit.*

Exception II.

There are also neuter nouns in *us*. Some change the ending *us* into *oris* for the genitive ; others, into *eris*. (See rules on the genders.) Lastly, some have the genitive in *uris* [1].

1. Neuter substantives in *us*, genitive *oris.*

Singular.		Plural.	
N. Corpus,	*a body.*	N. Corpora,	*bodies.*
G. Corporis,	*of a body.*	G. Corporum,	*of bodies.*
D. Corpori,	*to a body.*	D. Corporibus,	*to bodies.*
A. Corpus,	*a body.*	A. Corpora,	*bodies.*
V. ô Corpus,	*o body.*	V. ô Corpora,	*o bodies.*
A. Corpore,	*from a body.*	A. Corporibus,	*from bodies.*

Decline thus:

Decus, *an ornament.*	Littus, *a shore.*
Facinus, *a great action.*	Nemus, *a forest.*
Fenus, *usury.*	Pectus, *the chest (bosom).*
Frigus, *cold.*	Tempus, *time.*

2. Neuter substantives in *us*, genitive *eris.*

N. Vulnus,	*a wound.*	N. Vulnera,	*wounds.*
G. Vulneris,	*of a wound.*	G. Vulnerum,	*of wounds.*
D. Vulneri,	*to a wound.*	D. Vulneribus,	*to wounds.*

---

[1] Ex. *Crus*, the leg, *cruris, cruri, crure ;* plural, *crura, crurum, cruribus.* See p. 53.

	Singular.		Plural.	
A. Vulnus,	a wound.	A. Vulnera,	wounds.
V. ô Vulnus,	o wound.	V. ô Vulnera,	o wounds.
A. Vulnere,	from a wound.	A. Vulneribus,	from wounds.

Decline thus:

Fœdus, *a treaty.*	Onus, *a load.*
Funus, *a funeral.*	Opus, *a work.*
Genus, *a family.*	Pondus, *a weight.*
Latus, *the side.*	Scelus, *a crime.*
Munus, *an office.*	Sidus, *a star.*

Obs. There are also neuter substantives in *er ;* but they fall within the rule of the regular declension, and must be considered as merely ending in *r ;* since the noun in itself forms the root, and merely adds *is* to the genitive, and the regular endings in the other cases. Ex.: *Cadaver,* a dead body, *cadaveris, cadaveri, cadavere :* plural, *cadavera, cadaverum, cadaveribus.*

Obs. There are three nouns which are declined in an irregular manner. They are as follows:

1.

N. Juppiter *or* Jupiter, *Jupiter.*	A. Jovem.
	V. Jupiter.
G. Jovis.	A. Jove.
D. Jovi.	Plur. Joves (*the other cases are wanting*).

D

2.

	Singular.			Plural.	
N. Bos,	an ox.	N. Boves,	oxen.
G. Bovis,	of an ox.	G. Boum,	of oxen.
D. Bovi,	to an ox.	D. Bubus or bobus,	to oxen.
A. Bovem,	an ox.	A. Boves,	oxen.
V. ô Bos,	o ox.	V. ô Boves,	o oxen.
A. Bove,	from an ox.	A. Bubus or bobus,	from oxen.

3. *Sus*, a hog, genitive *suis*, has the dative and ablative plural *subus* for *suibus*.

DECLENSION OF COMPOUND SUB-STANTIVES.

Rule. Substantives composed of two nouns are declined like simple substantives, when only one of the nouns forming the compound is in the nominative case ; but when the compound substantive is formed of two nominative cases, both nouns are declined.

EXAMPLES.

1. Of a compound noun formed of a nominative and of another case.

	Singular.		Plural.
N. Senatusconsultum,	a senatus-consultum.	N. Senatusconsulta, senatus-consulta.
G. Senatusconsulti,	of a senatus-consultum.	G. Senatusconsultorum, of senatus-consulta.

Singular.	Plural.
D. Senatusconsulto, *to a* *senatus-consultum.*	D. Senatusconsultis, *to* *senatus-consulta.*
A. Senatusconsultum, *a* *senatus-consultum.*	A. Senatusconsulta, *sena-* *tus-consulta.*
V. ô Senatusconsultum, *o* *senatus-consultum.*	V. ô Senatusconsulta, *o* *senatus-consulta.*
A. Senatusconsulto, *from* *a senatus-consultum.*	A. Senatusconsultis, *from* *senatus-consulta.*

2. Of a noun composed of two nominative cases.

N. Respublica, *a republic.*	N. Respublicæ, *republics.*
G. Reipublicæ, *of a re-*publics.	G. Rerumpublicarum, *of* *republics.*
D. Reipublicæ, *to a re-*public.	D. Rebuspublicis, *to re-*publics.
A. Rempublicam, *a re-*public.	A. Respublicas, *republics.*
V. ô Respublica, *o republic.*	V. ô Respublicæ, *o repub-*lics.
A. Republica, *from a re-*public.	A. Rebuspublicis, *from* *republics.*

COMPOUND SUBSTANTIVES.

To serve as examples to the preceding rules.

1. Paterfamilias[2](familias, ancient genitive, for familiæ), *a father of a family.*	1. Plebiscitum, *a decree.* 2. Jusjurandum, *an oath.* 2. Rosmarinus, *rosemary.*

[2] In this example, it is the first noun, *pater*, that is declined.

FOURTH DIVISION.

Declension of Substantives of Greek origin.

Although substantives of Greek origin have in the nominative Greek terminations, and are mostly proper names, they generally take Latin endings in the oblique cases. According to the declension to which they belong in Greek, they are declined like Latin nouns, having the genitive case in *is*, or like those having their genitive in *æ*. A small number have the genitive in *i*.

The principal terminations of Greek substantives having the genitive in *is* are : *ma, i, an, in, on, or, y, yn, yr, ys, yx, inx, ynx.* Add to these the terminations *es, as, is, os, o,* which also belong to purely Latin nouns.

Substantives of Greek origin ending in *e*, as well as some ending in *as* and *es*, have the genitive in *æ*.

The genitive in *i* only belongs to nouns ending in the nominative in *os, eus, ous,* and *on.*

The declension of nouns of Greek origin does not differ from the Latin declension in the plural; the only differences are in the singular for masculine nouns in *as* and *es*, genitive *æ*, for masculine nouns in *eus* and *os*, and for feminine nouns in *e* and *o*. As to other nouns, they are declined exactly like Latin substantives, with a few peculiarities in the various plural and singular cases to be mentioned hereafter.

I. MASCULINE.

EXAMPLES.

1. Of a masculine substantive of Greek origin, ending in *as*.

Singular.		*Plural.*	
N. Tiar*as*,	*a turban.*	N. Tiar*æ*,	*turbans.*
G. Tiar*æ*,	*of a turban.*	G. Tiar*arum*,	*of turbans.*
D. Tiar*æ*,	*to a turban.*	D. Tiar*is*,	*to turbans.*
A. Tiar*an*,	*a turban.*	A. Tiar*as*,	*turbans.*
V. ô Tiar*a*,	*o turban.*	V. ô Tiar*æ*,	*o turbans.*
A. Tiar*a*,	*from a turban.*	A. Tiar*is*,	*from turbans.*

2. Of a substantive masculine of Greek origin ending in *es*.

N. Dynast*es*,	*a ruler.*	N. Dynast*æ*,	*rulers.*
G. Dynast*æ*,	*of a ruler.*	G. Dynast*arum*,	*of rulers.*
D. Dynast*æ*,	*to a ruler.*	D. Dynast*is*,	*to rulers.*
A. Dynast*en*,	*a ruler.*	A. Dynast*as*,	*rulers.*
V. ô Dynast*e*,	*o ruler.*	V. ô Dynast*æ*,	*o rulers.*
A. Dynast*e*,	*from a ruler.*	A. Dynast*is*,	*from rulers.*

Obs. Many proper names in *es*, especially those in *des, les, cles, tes,* have the genitive case in *is*, the dative in *i*, the accusative in *em*. Thus are declined: *Alcibiades, Astyages, Apelles, Euclides, Euphrates, Euripides, Cambyses, Miltiades, Simonides, Phraates, Xerxes, Æschines,* &c. But the accusative case of these nouns is more frequently *en* than *em*.

Patronymic names, as *Æneades,* son or descendant of Æneas, are all declined like the example given above.

3. Of a masculine substantive of Greek origin in *eus.* These nouns are declined in two ways.

A.		B.	
N. Orph*eus,*	*Orpheus.*	N. Orph*eus,*	*Orpheus.*
G. Orph*ei,*	*of Orpheus.*	G. Orph*ei,* or Orph*i,*	*of Orpheus.*
D. Orph*eo,*	*to Orpheus.*	D. Orph*ei,* or Orph*i,*	*to Orpheus.*
A. Orph*eum,*	*Orpheus.*	A. Orph*ea,*	*Orpheus.*
V. ô Orph*eu,*	*o Orpheus.*	V. ô Orph*eu,*	*o Orpheus.*
A. Orph*eo, from Orpheus.*		A. Orph*eo, from Orpheus.*	

4. Of a substantive masculine of Greek origin ending in *os.*

N. Ath*os,* the name of a mountain.	A. Ath*on,* or Ath*onem,*	
	V. ô Ath*os,*	
G. Ath*o,*	A. Ath*o,* or Ath*one.*	
D. Ath*o,*		

Obs. Some nouns ending in *os* (Latin *us*) have the Greek accusative in *on.* Ex.: *Scorpios,* a scorpion; accusative *scorpion.*

GREEK MASCULINE NOUNS.

To serve as examples to the preceding rules.

1. *as.* Æneas.
   Andreas, *Andrew.*
   Archias.
   Boreas, *the north wind.*
   Epaminondas.

1. *as.* Eurotas, *the Eurotas.*
   Hermagoras.
   Midas.
   Perdiccas.
   Protagoras.
   Pythagoras.

2. *es.* Alcides.
   Anagnostes, *a reader.*
   Epirotes, *an Epirote.*
   Geometres, *a mathematician.*
   Olympinices, *a victor in the Olympic games.*
   Pelides, *a son of Peleus.*

2. *es.* Anchises.
   Cometes, *a comet.*

   Planetes, *a planet.*
   Priamides, *a son of Priam.*
   Pyrites, *a flint.*
   Satrapes, *a satrap.*
   Sophistes, *a sophist.*
   Tydides, *a son of Tydeus.*

3. *eus.* Idomeneus.
   Peleus.
   Phalereus, *of Phalerii.*

3. *eus.* Prometheus.
   Theseus.
   Tydeus.

4. *os.* Androgeos.

II. FEMININE NOUNS.

EXAMPLES.

1. Of a feminine substantive of Greek origin in *e*.

Singular.	Plural.
N. Epitom*e*, *an abridge-* *ment.*	N. Epitom*æ*, *abridge-* *ments.*
G. Epitom*es*, *of an abridge-* *ment.*	G. Epitom*arum*, *of* *abridgements.*
D. Epitom*æ*, *to an abridge-* *ment.*	D. Epitom*is*, *to abridge-* *ments.*
A. Epitom*en*, *an abridge-* *ment.*	A. Epitom*as*, *abridge-* *ments.*
V. ô Epitom*e*, *o abridge-* *ment.*	V. ô Epitom*æ*, *o abridge-* *ments.*
A. Epitom*e*, *from an ab-* *ridgement.*	A. Epitom*is*, *from* *abridgements.*

2. Of a substantive feminine of Greek origin in *o* :
they are all proper names.

N.   Ech*o*.

G.   Ech*us.*

D.

A.

V. } Ech*o*.

A.

GREEK FEMININE NOUNS.

To serve as examples to the preceding rules.

Aloe, *aloes.*	Clio.
Circe.	Crambe, *a cabbage.*

Danae.

Dido.

Grammatice, *grammar*.

Musice, *music*.

Phœnice.

Rhetorice, *rhetoric*.

Sappho.

III. NEUTER NOUNS.

Neuter nouns of Greek origin have their ending in *on* (genitive *i*), *i*, *y*, and *ma* (genitive *is*). Ex.: *symposium*, a feast; *sinapi*, mustard; *misy*, the truffle; *poema*, a poem. But as these neuter nouns, with very few differences shown below, are declined exactly like Latin nouns, we shall merely refer to the declension of the latter.

Remarks on some cases of Greek nouns having the genitive case in is.

For substantives which have *is* in the genitive, we often find, (especially in poetry,) Greek forms, particularly in the following examples:

1. *Singular.*

a) In the genitive singular the poets often give to nominative cases ending in *is* the Greek genitive *idos* instead of the Latin *idis*. Ex.: *Atlantis*, genitive *Atlantidos*; *Daphnis*, genitive *Daphnidos*; *Phasis*, genitive *Phasidos*.

The same change takes place in words ending in *as*, *ys*, and *y*, of which the Greek genitive is *ados* or *os*. Ex.: *Misy*, genitive *Misyos*; *Pallas*, genitive *Pallados*; *Tethys*, genitive *Tethyos*. For *Peleus* and *Theseus* we find *Peleos* and *Theseos;* whereas in prose these nouns are declined like *Orpheus.* (See page 42, declension of masculine substantives in *eus.*) *Pan* (the god) has *Panos,* even in prose, to distinguish it from *panis,* genitive *panis,* bread.

Feminine substantives in *sis* often take *seos.* Ex.: *Basis,* a basis, *mathesis,* mathematics, *poesis,* poetry, *ellipsis,* an ellipsis; genitive *baseos, matheseos, poeseos,* and *ellipseos.*

Proper names in *es,* especially those in *cles,* often take *i;* thus, *Agathocli, Diocli, Pericli, Procli, Themistocli,* from *Agathocles, Diocles, Pericles, Procles, Themistocles.* *Achilli* and *Ulixi* are probably contractions of *Achillei* and *Ulixei,* from *Achilleus* and *Ulixeus.* (See the declension of *Orpheus,* p. 42.)

b) In the accusative the poets prefer employing the Greek ending *a.* Ex.: *Agamemnona, Cyclopa, Helicona, heroa, Memnona ;* from *Agamemnon, Cyclops, Helicon, heros, Memnon.* *Aer,* the air, and *æther,* ether, have *aera* and *æthera* in prose also. *Pan* has *Pana* to distinguish it from *panem,* accusative of *panis,* bread.

Nouns in *is* (Latin accusative *im*) and in *ys* have sometimes the accusative in *in* and *yn* (Greek accusative *ιν* and *υν*) instead of *im* and *ym.* Ex.: *Agin, Halyn, Nabin, Tigrin.*

Proper names in *es,* genitive *is,* are declined in the accusative like those in *es,* genitive *æ,* as mentioned above. (P. 41.)

c) The vocative is generally like the nominative,

but the nouns ending in *s* reject this letter, as we have already seen in the declension of *Orpheus.* Thus *Cotys, Daphnis, Phyllis, Thaïs,* have their vocative *Coty, Daphni, Phylli, Thaï.*

Nouns in *as*, genitive *antis*, have the vocative in *a.* Ex.: *Atlas,* genitive *Atlantis,* vocative *Atla. Calchas,* genitive *Calchantis,* vocative *Calcha.*

Proper names in *es*, genitive *is*, have sometimes *e* in the vocative. Ex.: *Achille, Carneade, Damocle, Pericle, Sophocle.*

d) Greek nouns of which the accusative ends in *im* or *in* have the ablative in *i.* Ex.: *Poesi, Neapoli.*

2. *Plural.*

a) The genitive plural sometimes has the Greek ending *on*, especially in the titles of books. Ex.: *Epigrammaton, metamorphoseon,* instead of *epigrammatum* and *metamorphosium.*

Epodon, Georgicon, Satyricon, instead of *Epodorum, Georgicorum, Satyricorum,* are exceptions belonging to masculine nouns in *us*, genitive *i*, and neuter nouns in *um*, genitive *i.*

b) For the dative plural, the Greek termination *si* or *sin* is rare, and only employed by the poets. Ex.: *Lemniasi, Troasin,* from *Lemniades, Troades.*

Neuter nouns in *ma*, genitive *matis*, have the dative and ablative in *is* instead of *ibus;* thus *poema* has *poematis* instead of *poematibus.* These nouns of Greek origin are neuter, and the only nouns in *a* which have the genitive in *is.*

Decline thus: *Ænigma,* an enigma; *diploma,* a

diploma; *emblema,* an emblem; *epigramma,* an epi-
gram; *hypomnema,* a commentary; *paradigma,* an
example.

c) The accusative plural in *as* instead of *es* is
used for all nouns that have that accusative in the
Greek declension. Ex.: *Æthiopas, Arcadas, aspidas,
Cyclopas, phalangas, pyramidas,* from *Æthiops,* an
Ethiop; *Arcas,* an Arcadian; *aspis,* a shield; *Cyclops,*
a Cyclop; *phalanx,* a phalanx; *pyramis,* a pyramid.

Table of the Classification of Substantives having is *in
the Genitive Singular.*

1st Class.   Nouns ending in a consonant.

Terminations.		Examples.		Exceptions.
N.	Gen.	Nom.	Gen.	
c	cis	halec	halecis, *the herring*	See p. 50.
l	lis	animal	animalis, *an animal*	,, 50.
en	inis	carmen	carminis, *a song*	,, 50.
r	ris	calcar	calcaris, *a spur*	,, 50.

s 1. preceded by a vowel.

as	atis	æstas	æstatis, *summer*	,, 51.
es	is	nubes	nubis, *a cloud*	,, 51.
es	itis	miles	militis, *a soldier*	,, 51.
is	is	canis	canis, *a dog*	,, 52.
os	oris	os	oris, *the mouth*	,, 53.
us	eris	genus	generis, *a gender*	,, 53.
	oris	corpus	corporis, *the body*	,, 53.
	uris	tellus	telluris, *the earth*	,, 54.
aus	audis	laus	laudis, *praise*	,, 54.

Termina-tions.		Examples.		Exceptions.
N.	Gen.	Nom.	Gen.	

s 2. preceded by a consonant.

ls	ltis	puls	pultis, *porridge*	See p. 54.
ms	mis	hiems	hiemis, *winter*	,, 54.
ns	ntis	frons	frontis, *the forehead*	,, 54.
rs	rtis	pars	partis, *a part*	,, 54.
bs	bis	plebs	plebis, *the people*	,, 54.
ps	pis	stips	stipis, *profit*	,, 54.
t	tis	caput	capitis, *the head*	,, 55.
x	cis	pax	pacis, *peace*	,, 55.
ex	icis	judex	judicis, *a judge*	,, 55.
ix	icis	radix	radicis, *a root*	,, 55.
ox	ocis	vox	vocis, *the voice*	,, 56.
ux	ucis	dux	ducis, *a chief*	,, 56.
yx	ycis	calyx	calycis, *a bud*	,, 56.
	ygis	Styx	Stygis, *the Styx*	,, 56.

2nd Class. Nominative case ending in a vowel.

a	atis	poema	poematis, *a poem*	,, 56.
e	is	mare	maris, *the sea*	,, 56.
o	inis	ordo	ordinis, *order*	,, 56.
	onis	leo	leonis, *a lion*	,, 57.
	onis	Macedo	Macedonis, *a Mace-donian*	,, 57.

REMARKS ON SOME CASES OF SUBSTANTIVES
HAVING *is* IN THE GENITIVE.

1. Genitive singular.

The nominative singular of substantives having *is*

E

in the genitive, has, as we have seen, very different
terminations, viz.: the consonants *l, n, r, s, x* (rarely
c and *t*) and the vowels *a* [3], *e*, and *o*.

But as the genitive cannot always be formed by
adding merely *is*, the preceding table shows the classification of substantives according to the final letter
of the nominative, with the genitive proper to each.
We shall review these several classes, and note the
chief exceptions.

1st CLASS.—NOMINATIVES ENDING BY CONSONANTS.

c,   This termination only contains the two words
        halec, the herring, gen. *halecis*, and *lac*, milk,
        gen. *lactis*.

l, gen. *is.* Ex.: *animal*, an animal, gen. *animalis*.
        EXCEPTIONS: *mel*, honey; *fel*, gall; which
        double the consonant *l*: *mellis, fellis.*

en, gen. *inis.* Ex.: *carmen*, a song, gen. *carminis.*
        EXCEPTIONS: *attagen*, the heath-cock; *lichen*,
        lichen; *lien* and *splen*, the gall; *ren*, the back;
        which have *enis.*

r, gen. *is.* Ex.: *calcar*, a spur, gen. *calcaris; amor*,
        love, gen. *amoris.* EXCEPTIONS:
        1. In *ar: far*, wheat, gen. *farris; hepar*, the
        liver, gen. *hepatis.*
        2. In *er:* nouns in *ber* and *ter*, gen. *bris* and

---

[3] Nouns of Greek origin in *ma*, neuter, are the only substantives
ending in *a* which have *is* (*matis*) in the genitive.

tris: as *imber*, rain ; *pater*, a father[4]. *Iter*, a way, has the genitive *itineris*.

3. In *or: cor*, the heart, which has the gen. *cordis*.

4. In *ur: ebur*, ivory, *eboris; femur*, the thigh, *femoris; jecur*, the liver, *jecoris (jocineris, jocinoris,* and *jecinoris); robur*, the green oak, *roboris*.

s,   *a*) preceded by a vowel.

as, gen. *atis.* Ex.: *æstas*, summer, gen. *æstatis.* EXCEPTIONS : *anas*, a duck, gen. *anatis (a* short)*; as*, a penny, *assis; mas*, a male, *maris; vas*, bail, *vadis; vas*, a vase, *vasis.*

Greek nouns are declined as in Greek. Ex.: *Pallas, Palladis; elephas*, an elephant; *gigas*, a giant; *elephantis, gigantis; artocreas*, a meat-pie, *artocreatis.*

es, gen. *is.* Ex.: *nubes*, a cloud, gen. *nubis.* None of these nouns are personal nouns.

es, gen. *itis.* Ex.: *miles*, a soldier, gen. *militis.* These substantives mostly belong to the occupations of men. A few nouns not having this signification are declined in the same way : *cespes*, a turf; *fomes*, fuel; *gurges*, an abyss; *limes*, a path; *merges*, a sheaf;

---

[4] But we see here that it is merely owing to the rejection of the *e* in the root, as we observed p. 15.

palmes, a vine-root; *stipes,* a stake; *trames,*
a path.

EXCEPTIONS.

1. Gen. *etis* (*e* short): *abies,* the fir; *aries,*
   a ram; *interpres,* an interpreter; *paries,* a
   wall; *seges,* a crop; *teges,* a mat of osier.

2. Have *etis* (*e* long): *inquies,* anxiety; *quies*
   and *requies,* repose, which also have *re-
   quiem* and *requie* in the accusative and ablative; and the three Greek substantives,
   lebes, a cauldron; *magnes,* the magnet;
   tapes, a carpet.

3. Gen. *idis:* *obses,* an hostage; *præses,* a
   president.

4. Gen. *edis* (*e* short): *pes,* the foot, and its
   compounds.

5. Gen. *edis* (*e* long): *heres,* an heir, and
   merces, a reward. Remark also: *bes,* eight
   ounces, gen. *bessis; Ceres* (name of the
   goddess), *Cereris; æs,* brass, *æris; præs,* a
   respondent, *prædis.*

is, gen. *is.* Ex.: *canis,* a dog, gen. *canis.*

EXCEPTIONS.

1. Gen. *idis:* *ægis,* the ægis; *cassis,* a
   helmet; *capis,* a vase with two handles;
   cuspis, a point; *lapis,* a stone; *proboscis,* the proboscis; *promulsis,* the entrance
   to the table; *pyramis,* a pyramid; *tigris,*

a tiger; therefore the genitive is *tigridis*, *ægidis*, &c.

2. Gen. *itis*: *lis*, a lawsuit; *Dis*, the god Pluto; *Samnis*, a Samnite; *Quiris*, a Quirite; gen. *litis*, *Ditis*, &c.

3. Gen. *eris*: *cinis*, ashes; *pulvis*, dust; *cucumis*, a cucumber; *vomis*, a ploughshare; gen. *cineris*, *pulveris*, &c.

Remark also: *glis*, a dormouse, gen. *gliris;* *sanguis*, blood, gen. *sanguinis;* *semis*, a half-penny, gen. *semissis*.

os, gen. *oris*. Ex.: *os*, the mouth, gen. *oris*.

EXCEPTIONS.

Gen. *otis*: *cos*, a grinding-stone; *dos*, a dower; *nepos*, a grandson; *sacerdos*, a priest; gen. *cotis*, *dotis*, &c.

Custos, a keeper, has *custodis;* *bos*, an ox, *bovis;* *os*, a bone, *ossis*.

Greek nouns in *os* have the genitive in *ois*. Ex.: *Heros*, a hero, gen. *herois*. Others in *os*, as *Argos*, *epos*, only have the nominative and accusative.

us, gen. *eris*. Ex.: *genus*, gender, gen. *generis*.

gen. *oris*. Ex.: *corpus*, the body, gen. *corporis*.

EXCEPTIONS.

1. Gen. *uis*: *grus*, a stork; *sus*, a pig; gen. *gruis*, *suis*.

2. Gen. *uris*: *crus*, the thigh; *jus*, law; *mus*,

E 3

a mouse; *pus*, matter; *rus*, the country; *tellus*, the earth ; *tus*, incense.

3. Gen. *utis : juventus*, youth; *salus*, safety; *senectus*, old age; *servitus*, servitude; *virtus*, virtue.

4. Gen. *udis : incus*, an anvil; *palus*, a marsh; *subscus*, a dove-tail.

5. *Pecus*, an ewe, has *pecudis* (*u* short), but *pecoris* when it means sheep.

6. *Venus* (the goddess) has *Veneris*.

7. Greek proper nouns ending in *us* have *untis*. Ex.: *Selinus, Selinuntis*. But *tripus*, a tripod; *Œdipus*, Œdipus, and those of a similar formation, have *podis*, whence *tripodis*, &c.

aus, gen. *audis*. Ex.: *laus*, praise, and *fraus*, deceit; the only two words of this termination.

s,   *b*) preceded by a consonant.

ls ⎫
ns ⎬ change *s* into *tis*.
rs ⎭

Ex.: *pars*, a part, gen. *partis; puls*, porridge, *pultis ; frons*, the forehead, *frontis*. EXCEPTIONS: *Frons*, foliage ; *glans*, an acorn; *juglans*, a walnut-tree; gen. *frondis, glandis, juglandis*.

ms. One word only, *hiems*, winter, gen. *hiemis*.

bs, gen. *bis*. Ex.: *plebs*, the people, *plebis*.

ps, gen. *pis*. Ex.: *stips*, profit, *stipis*.

Obs. Nouns ending in *ceps*, derived from the verb *capere*, to take, have *cipis*. Ex.:

princeps, a prince, *principis.* One only, *auceps,* a bird-catcher, has *aucupis.* Those that are derived from *caput,* the head, have *capitis.* (See declension of adjectives.)

t. One noun only has this ending: *caput,* the head, gen. *capitis.*

x, gen. altered to *cis.* Ex.: *pax,* peace, *pacis.*

ex, gen. altered to *icis.* Ex.: *judex,* a judge, *judicis.*

EXCEPTIONS:

1. Gen. *ecis* (*e* long): *nex,* death; *fœnisex,* a mower; *resex,* the principal thread.
2. *ecis* (*e* short): *halex,* a herring, and *vervex,* a sheep.
3. *egis* (*e* short): *aquilex,* a fountain maker; *grex,* a flock; *Lelex,* the name of a people, the Lelegi.
4. *egis* (*e* long): *rex,* a king, and *lex,* law, and their compounds.
5. *igis: remex,* a rower, *remigis.*

Observe besides, *senex,* an old man, which has the genitive *senis; supellex,* household goods, gen. *supellectilis; vibex,* a scion, *vibicis.*

ix, gen. altered to *icis* (*i* long). Ex.: *Radix,* a root, *radicis.*

EXCEPTIONS:

Gen. *icis* (*i* short): *calix,* a cup; *cilix,* an hair-shirt; *coxendix,* the hip; *filix,* fern; *fulix,* the moor-hen; *fornix,* an arch; *hystrix,*

a porcupine ; *larix*, the larinx ; *natrix*, a serpent ; *pix*, pitch ; *salix*, a willow ; *varix*, a
varicose vein.

Observe also : *nix*, snow, gen. *nivis*, and
strix, a sort of night bird, gen. *strigis*.

ox, gen. *ocis*. Ex. : *vox*, the voice, gen. *vocis*.

ux, gen. *ucis* (*u* short). *Dux*, a chief, gen. *ducis*.

EXCEPTIONS :

Gen. *ucis* (*u* long) : *lux*, light, and *Pollux*.
ugis (*u* short) : *conjux*, a wife.
ugis (*u* long) : *frux*, fruit.

yx, Greek termination, which has the genitive as
in Greek. Ex. : *bombyx*, the silk worm, has
bombycis ; calyx, a bud, has *calycis*. *Japyx,
Phryx, Styx,* have *Japygis, Phrygis, Stygis.
Onyx* has *onychis*. *Phalanx, syrinx,* and
sphinx have the genitive in *gis ;* hence *phalangis,*
&c.

2ND CLASS. NOMINATIVE ENDING BY VOWELS.

ma, gen. *matis*. Ex. : *poema*, a poem, gen. *poematis*.

e, gen. *is*. Ex. : *mare*, the sea, gen. *maris*.

o, gen. *inis :* genitive regular of all common nouns
ending in *do* and *go*. Ex. : *ordo*, order,
gen. *ordinis ; margo*, the margin, gen. *mar-
ginis*.

EXCEPTIONS :

Gen. *onis :* *udo*, a shoe ; *cudo*, a helmet ; *ligo*,
a hoe ; *harpago*, a harpoon ; *unedo*, the sloe ;
prædo, a thief.

gen. *onis* (*o* long). Genitive regular of all the
other nouns in *o* and *io*. Ex.: *leo*, a lion, gen.
leonis; ratio, reason, gen. *rationis*. Proper
names of men in *o*. Ex.: *Plato*, Plato, gen.
Platonis. Those in *o* answering to Greek
nouns in ων, οντος, have the genitive in *ontis*.
Ex.: *Antipho, Antiphontis*.   EXCEPTIONS:
homo, a man; *nemo*, nobody; *turbo*, a whirlwind; *Apollo*, Apollo, have *hominis, neminis,
turbinis, Apollinis*.

gen. *onis* (*o* short). Genitive regular, of the greater
number of names of people. Ex.: *Macedo*, a
Macedonian, gen. *Macedonis*. EXCEPTIONS
(*o* long): *Iones*, the Ionians; *Lacones*, the
Spartans.

Observe besides: *caro*, meat, which has the
genitive *carnis*, and *Anio*, the Teverone,
Anienis.

gen. *us*. Only for Greek proper names of women.
Ex.: *Dido*, gen. *Didus*.

Obs. Terminations in *i*, *y* belong exclusively to Greek substantives.

OTHER CASES TAKING THE LETTER *i*.

Accusative singular im *instead of* em.

Many nouns in *is*, gen. *is*, have the accusative
singular in *im* instead of *em*, viz.:

1. All Greek nouns, or nouns of Greek origin in
is, which in the latter language have the accusative

in *ιυ*. See the declension of Greek nouns, particular remarks on the accusative, p. 46.

2. Proper names of rivers and towns: *Albis*, the Elbe; *Athesis*, the Adige; *Bætis*, the Bætis; *Tiberis*, the Tiber.

3. Common Latin nouns: *amussis*, a measuring rule; *ravis*, hoarseness; *sitis*, thirst; *tussis*, a cough; *vis*, strength, have the accusative constantly in *im*.

Obs. Febris, fever; *pelvis*, a basin; *puppis*, the poop; *restis*, a cord; *securis*, a hatchet; *turris*, a tower, have more frequently *im* than *em*.

Ablative singular i *instead of* e.

A certain number of nouns having the genitive in *is* have the ablative singular in *i* instead of *e*. They are as follows:

1. All nouns having the accusative in *im* instead of *em*.

EXCEPTION: *restis*, a cord, which has oftener *reste*.

Obs. Nouns admitting of *em* also in the accusative do not always exclude the ending in *e*.

2. Neuter nouns in *e, al, ar*. Ex.: *mare*, the sea, ablative *mari;* likewise *calcar*, a spur; *vectigal*, a toll.

EXCEPTIONS: 1. *Far*, flour; *baccar*, a flask; *hepar*, gen. *hepatis*, the liver; *jubar*, a brilliant; *nectar*, nectar; *sal*, salt, which have the ablative in *e*.

2. Names of towns ending in *e* never admit of any

other termination but *e* in the ablative. Ex.: *Præ-neste, Cære, Reate.*

Obs. Rete, a net, has *rete* and *reti; rus*, gen. *ruris*, the country, has *rure* and *ruri.*

3. Names of months in *is* and *er*, and substantives in *is* which originally were adjectives.

Ex.: *Aprilis*, April; *September, October, November, December*, and *Sextilis*, August; likewise *æqualis*, an equal; *affinis*, a neighbour; *annalis*, a book of annals; *bipennis*, an axe; *canalis*, a canal; *familiaris*, a familiar friend; *gentilis*, the heathen; *molaris*, a molar tooth; *natalis*, a birthday; *rivalis*, a rival; *popularis*, a compatriot; *sodalis*, a companion; *strigilis*, a curry-comb; *triremis*, a three-oared galley; *vocalis*, a vowel.

EXCEPTIONS: 1. *Juvenis*, a youth, has always *e* in the ablative.

2. When these adjectives have become proper names, they always take *e* in the ablative. Ex.: *Martialis*, ablative *Martiale.*

Obs. The following are often employed with *i: amnis*, a river; *avis*, a bird; *civis*, a citizen; *classis*, a fleet; *fustis*, a stick; *ignis*, fire; *imber*, a shower; *orbis*, the globe; *unguis*, a claw or nail; *vesper*, the evening.

Genitive plural *ium* instead of *um*.

General Rule. Parisyllabic[s] nouns have the

---

[s] Viz., nouns having the same number of syllables in the nominative and genitive singular.

genitive in *ium*, and imparisyllabic[6] nouns have *um*.

Observations. The following have *ium* instead of *um* :—

I. All nouns which in the ablative singular have *i* instead of *e*, especially neuter nouns in *e, al, ar*, which have *ia* in the nominative plural. Ex.: *animal, calcar, mare*, gen. *animalium, calcarium, marium*.

II. The parisyllabic nouns. 1. In *es*. Ex.: *nubes*, a cloud, *nubium*.

2. In *is*. Ex.: *civis*, a citizen, *civium*.

3. In *er*. Ex.: *imber*, rain; *linter*, a boat; *venter*, the belly; *uter*, a wine-skin, which have *imbrium*, &c.

Note. *Caro*, meat, has *carnium*.

Quiris, a Quirite, and *Samnis*, a Samnite, though imparisyllabic, have *Quiritium, Samnitium*.

EXCEPTIONS: The following nouns have *um* in the genitive :—

1. In *es* : *vates*, a diviner, and *strues*, a heap.

2.   *is* : *canis*, a dog; *panis*, bread; *juvenis*, a youth; *mensis*, a month; *sedes*, a seat.

3.   *er* : *pater*, a father; *frater*, a brother; *mater*, a mother; *accipiter*, a hawk.

4.   *senex* (gen. *senis*), an old man, has *senum*.

---

[6] Viz., nouns having fewer syllables in the nominative than in the genitive singular.

III. Nouns ending in *s* and *x* preceded by a consonant, whereas those in *s* and *x* preceded by a vowel, have the genitive in *um*. Ex.: *arx*, a citadel; *cliens*, a client; *cohors*, a cohort; *dens*, a tooth; *mons*, a mountain; which have *montium, dentium*, &c.

EXCEPTIONS:

1. *Lynx, sphinx*, and *opes*, riches, have *lyncum, sphingum*, and *opum*.

2. *Arpinas*, a native of Arpinum, and *Fidenas*, a Fidenate, have *Arpinatium* and *Fidenatium*.

3. *Penates*, household gods, and *optimates* (no singular), have *penatium* and *optimatium*.

4. The other nouns in *as*, gen. sing. *atis*, have generally *atum*, although *atium* is used also.

5. The following substantives ending in *s* and *x*, preceded by a vowel, have *ium* instead of *um; as*, a Roman penny, *assium; glis*, a rat, *glirium; lis*, a lawsuit, *litium; mas*, a male, *marium; os*, a bone, *ossium; vis*, strength, *virium;* and generally *fraus*, fraud, and *mus*, a mouse, *fraudium, murium; fauces* (from the obsolete singular *faux*), an abyss, *faucium; nix*, snow, *nivium; strix*, the screech-owl, *strigium; nox*, night, *noctium*.

Obs. The names of the feast days ending in *alia*, only employed in the plural, have the genitive also in *orum;* thus, from *bacchanalia*, the feast of Bacchus, we have *bacchanaliorum;* from *compitalia*,

the feast of the god of the crossways, *compitaliorum*;
from *saturnalia*, the feast of Saturn, *saturnaliorum*;
from *sponsalia*, the feast of betrothel, *sponsaliorum*;
besides the common nouns *ancile*, a shield, and
vectigal, a toll, have *anciliorum, vectigaliorum*.

FIFTH DIVISION.

IRREGULARITIES IN DECLENSION.

I. *Undeclinable Substantives.*

1. Greek substantives in *i* and *y* are undeclinable.
Ex.: *gummi*, gum; *asty*, a city.

Except the compounds of *meli*, honey. Ex.: *hydromeli* (gen. *itos*), mead.

2. The names of the letters of the alphabet in
Greek and Latin.

3. The words *pondo*, a pound; *cæpe*, an onion; *fas*,
right (law); *git*, cumin; *instar*, equality; *nefas*,
wrong (injury); *semis*, half.

4. All words which, without being substantives,
are employed as such. Ex.: Triste illud *vale*, this
sad farewell.

5. Many biblical proper names which have no
Latin termination. Ex.: *Adam, Jacob, Isaac*, &c.

Obs. However, to decline them, a Latin ending is often given them, as *Adamus, Jacobus.*

David, Daniel, Gabriel add *is* in the genitive.

As to those which have a termination like those employed in Latin, they are declined like Latin substantives. Ex.: *Josua,* gen. *Josuæ; Maria,* gen. *Mariæ; Moses,* gen. *Mosis. Jesus* has *Jesum* in the accusative, and *Jesu* in all the other cases.

6. All neuter nouns ending in *u* in all the cases of the singular.

II. *Substantives having no Plural.*

1. The following have no plural on account of their meaning:

a) Abstract nouns. Ex.: *justitia,* justice; *pietas,* piety; *pudor,* shame.

b) Nouns of matter. Ex.: *aurum,* gold; *sabulum,* sand; *sanguis,* blood.

c) Collective nouns. Ex.: *indoles,* the natural disposition of man; *scientia,* knowledge; *supellex,* a piece of furniture; *virus,* poison.

d) Proper names, unless persons of the same name or character are meant. Ex.: *Scipiones,* the Scipios, or men like one of the Scipios.

2. And the following:

Justitium, *a vacation.*	Specimen, *a specimen.*
Letum, *death.*	Ver, *spring.*
Meridies, *noon.*	Vesper, *evening.*

Obs. The following plural of a few abstract nouns are however met with in the best authors:

Adventus imperatorum, *the arrivals of generals.*

Omnes avaritiæ, *all avarice* (every sort of avarice).

Tres constantiæ, *three resolutions* (sorts of constantia).

Exitus bellorum, *the issues of wars.*

Industriæ, *haste.*

Invidiæ, *envy.*

Iracundiæ, *wrath.*

Mortes, *sorts of death, cases of death.*

Odia hominum, *hatred between men.*

Proceritates, *heights* (in a figurative sense).

Timores, *fears.*

Also:

Frigora, *cold.*
Grandines, *hail.*
Imbres, *showers.*

Nives, *snow.*
Soles, *sunshine.*

III. *Substantives with no Singular* [1].

a) The following:

Altaria, *an altar.*

Angustiæ, *a strait.*

Antes, *ranks* (of vines, &c.).

Argutiæ, *subtleness.*

Arma, *arms.*

Armamenta, *armament.*

Artus, *the limbs.*

Balneæ, *a bathing-house.*

Bigæ, *two horses in harness.*

Blanditiæ, *flatteries.*

Cani, *grey hairs.*

Cancelli, *iron gates.*

Casses, *nets.*

Castra, *a camp.*

---

[1] The greater part of these plural substantives are connected with a singular noun, belonging almost always to a different declension, or having a totally different meaning.

Cervices, *the nape of the neck.*

Clathri, *an iron gate.*

Clitellæ, *a pack-saddle.*

Codicilli, *tablets.*

Cœlites, *the blessed.*

Compedes, *handcuffs.*

Crates, *a hurdle.*

Crepundia, *playthings.*

Cunæ, *a cradle.*

Cunulæ, *id.*

Cunabula, *id.*

Incunabula, *id.*

Deliciæ, *delights.*

Diræ, *curses.*

Divitiæ, *riches.*

Epulæ, *victuals* (but epulum, *public banquet*).

Excubiæ, *a sentinel.*

Exsequiæ, *a funeral.*

Exta, *the intestines.*

Exuviæ, *the remains, skins of animals, dress.*

Facetiæ, *wit.*

Fasti, *the calendar.*

Fauces, *the throat.*

Feriæ, *a feast.*

Fides, *strings* (of a lyre).

Fori, *a row of seats.*

Gemini, *twins.*

Grates, *thanks.*

Habenæ, *reins of a horse.*

Ilia, *the bowels.*

Illecebræ, *bait* (for fish, &c.).

Incunabula, *see* Cunæ.

Induciæ, *a truce.*

Induviæ, *clothes.*

Ineptiæ, *nonsense.*

Inferi, *the inhabitants of hell; hell.*

Inferiæ, *sacrifices offered to the Manes.*

Inimicitiæ, *enmity.*

Insidiæ, *snares.*

Intestina, *the intestines.*

Justa, *see* Inferiæ.

Lamenta, *lamentations.*

Lapicidinæ, *quarries.*

Liberi, *children.*

Loculi, *a cupboard with compartments, a strong box.*

Lustra, *a den.*

Majores, *ancestors.*

Manes, *the Manes.*

Manubiæ, *a booty.*

Minæ, *threats.*

Mœnia, *walls, ramparts.*

Munia, *business.*

Nugæ, *jokes, nonsense.*

Nuptiæ, *nuptials.*

Obices, *a bolt.*

Obliviæ, *oblivion.*

Penates, *the Penates, household gods.*

Phaleræ, *trappings for horses.*

Posteri, *posterity, descendants.*

Præcordia, *the diaphragm.*

Præstigiæ, *prestige.*

Primitiæ, *first-fruits.*

Primores, *the principal people.*

Proceres, *id.*

Quadrigæ, *four horses in harness.*

Reliquiæ, *relics.*

Salinæ, *salt mines.*

Sata, *a sown field.*

Scalæ, *a ladder.*

Scopæ, *a broom.*

Sentes, *a bush of thorns.*

Serta, *a garland of flowers.*

Sordes, *dirt.*

Spolia, *booty, prey.*

Superi, *inhabitants of earth, gods of the earth (opposed to the* inferi). *

Tenebræ, *darkness.*

Thermæ, *hot baths.*

Tormina, *the cholic.*

Tricæ, *nonsense, fidgets.*

Trigæ, *three horses in harness.*

Utensilia, *food.*

Valvæ, *folding-doors.*

Vepres, *thorns.*

Verbera, *stripes, blows.*

Viscera (gen. *um*), *the intestines.*

Virgulta, *shrubs.*

Vindiciæ, *an assertion, proof.*

b) The names of days and feasts:

Calendæ, *the first of the month.*

Nonæ, *the fifth of the month.*

Idus, *the thirteenth (or fifteenth) of the month.*

Feriæ, *a feast day.*

Nundinæ, *a market day.*

Bacchanalia, *the feast of Bacchus.*

Saturnalia, *the feast of Saturn.*

And other names of feasts ending in *alia* and *ilia.*

c) Some names of peoples, tribes, societies, groups of islands, mountain chains. Ex.:

Aborigines, *aborigines.*
Ægates, *the Ægatian Isles.*
Alpes, *the Alps.*
Baleares, *the Balearic isles.*
Brigantes, *the Brigantes*
(*inhabitants of Bra-ganza*).
Luceres, *the Luceri* (*a por-tion of the Roman people*).
Salii, *the Salians.*

d) Many names of towns:

Argi, *Argos.*
Athenæ, *Athens.*
Delphi.
Gabii.
Leuctra.
Syracusæ, *Syracuse.*
Thebæ, *Thebes.*
Veji.

Obs. The following substantives have a different signification in the plural from that in the singular.

Singular.	Plural.
Ædes, *a temple.*	Ædes, *a house.*
Aqua, *water.*	Aquæ, *mineral waters.*
Auxilium, *assistance.*	Auxiliæ, (*a*) *auxiliary troops,* (*b*) *expedients.*
Bonum, *a benefit.*	Bona, *fortune.*
Carcer, *a prison.*	Carceres, *barriers.*
Caro, *flesh.*	Carnes, *pieces of flesh.*
Castrum, *a fortress.*	Castra, *a camp.*
Cera, *wax.*	Ceræ, *tablets.*
Comitium, *the place where the comitia are held.*	Comitia, *the comitia.*
Copia, *abundance.*	Copiæ, *troops.*
Cupedia, *greediness.*	Cupediæ, *dainties.*
Facultas, *permission.*	Facultates, *riches.*

Singular.	Plural.
Finis, *the end, limit.*	Fines, *territory.*
Fortuna, *happiness, luck.*	Fortunæ, *fortune, property.*
Gratia, *gratitude.*	Gratiæ, *thanks.*
Hortus, *a garden.*	Horti, *a) a garden, b) a country house.*
Impedimentum, *hindrance.*	Impedimenta, *a) hindrance, b) baggage.*
Lignum, *wood.*	Ligna, *a piece of wood.*
Ludus, *a game, a joke.*	Ludi, *a public game.*
Lustrum, *a space of five years.*	Lustra, *a den.*
Naris, *the nostril.*	Nares, *the nose.*
Natalis, *a birthday.*	Natales, *extraction.*
Odor, *smell.*	Odores, *perfumery.*
Opera, *work, labour.*	Operæ, *workmen.*
(Ops) Opis, *assistance.*	Opes, *power.*
Pars, *a part.*	Partes, *a) parts, b) a performance, c) a party.*
Rostrum, *a beak, a prow.*	Rostra, *the Roman tribune, which was adorned with the beaks of ships.*
Sal, *salt.*	Sales, *sallies (of wit).*
Tabula, *a plank.*	Tabulæ, *an account book, a document.*

IV. *Substantives that form the plural in an irregular manner.*

Singular.	Plural.
Clathrum, *an iron gate.*	Clathri.
Cœlum, *heaven.*	Cœli.
Frenum, *the bit (of a horse).*	Freni (*also* frena).

Singular.	Plural.
Jocus, *a joke.*	Joca.
Jugerum, *an acre.*	Jugera (gen. *jugerum,* dat. *jugeribus*).
Locus, *a place.*	Loca (but also *loci, passage in a book*).
Ostrea, *an oyster.*	Ostrea (but also *ostreæ*).
Porrum, *a leek.*	Porri.
Rastrum, *a hoe.*	Rastri (but also *rastra*).
Siser (neuter), *a parsnip.*	Siseres.
Tartarus, *Tartarus.*	Tartara.
Vas (gen. *vasis*), *a vase.*	Vasa (gen. *vasorum*).

Obs. **Balneum,** a bath; *epulum,* a public banquet; *forum,* the market-place, belonging to an irregular plural, change their meaning as well as number. See p. 64, plural nouns having no singular.

V. *Substantives deficient in one or several cases.*

1. The nominative singular is wanting or seldom employed in the following words.

Daps (gen. *dapis*), *a banquet.*	Pollis (gen. *pollinis*), *flour of wheat.*
Ditio (gen. *ditionis*), *dominion.*	Ops (gen. *opis*), *assistance.*
Frux (gen. *frugis*), *fruit.*	Vicis *or* vix (gen. *vicis*), *vicissitude.*
Internecio (gen. *internecionis*), *utter ruin.*	

2. The following substantives have only certain cases:

Fors, *chance,* nom. and abl. *forte* (generally an adverb, *by chance*). The plural is wanting.

Lues, nom., *an epidemic,* acc. *luem,* abl. *lue.* Plural wanting.

Nemo, *nobody, none;* dat. *nemini,* acc. *neminem.*

Ops (seldom used), *assistance,* gen. *opis,* acc. *opem,* abl. *ope* (for the plural see the list of nouns altering their

signification in the plural, p. 68).

Vices or vix (seldom used), *alteration, vicissitude,* gen. *vicis,* acc. *vicem,* abl. *vice.* In the plural, *vices, vicibus;* no gen.

Vis, *strength,* acc. *vim,* abl. *vi;* the plural, *vires, virium,* &c. is complete.

3. The following have only the ablative singular:

Sponte, generally employed with a possessive pronoun. Ex.: *Sua sponte,* of his own accord.

Jussu, *by command of.*

Mandatu, *according to commission.*

Natu, *of age.*

Rogatu, *on demand.*

Others are no longer to be found but in certain forms of speech. Ex.: *venum,* on sale; with the verb *dare,* to put up for sale; *nauci,* in the sentence *non nauci esse,* not to be worth a walnut shell.

4. The following have no genitive plural:

Cor, *the heart.*
Cos, *a grinding stone.*
Rus, *the country.*
Sal, *salt.*

Sol, *the sun.*
Vas (gen. *vadis*), *the respondant, bail.*

VI. *Substantives having several endings in the nominative case.*

Many substantives vary their declension, according to their endings in the nominative case. Several change their gender in changing their termination. The following are those most generally employed:

a) With the ending *us* (masc.) or *um* (neuter):

Baculus, baculum, *a stick.* *bow* (cubita, plur. meaning *cubits*).

Balteus, balteum, *a belt, a baldric.* Jugulus, jugulum, *the throat.*

Callus, callum, *callosity.* Intubus, intubum, *endive.*

Clypeus, clypeum, *a buckler.* Lupinus, lupinum, *lupine* (a sort of pulse).

Commentarius, commentarium, *a commentary.* Papyrus, papyrum, *papyrus.*

Cubitus, cubitum, *the el-* Porrus, porrum, *the leek.*

b) In *us*, gen. *us* (*u* long), masc., and *um*, neuter.

Angiportus, angiportum, *a lane.* Suggestus, suggestum, *a scene* (*of a theatre*).

Eventus, eventum, *an event.* Tonitrus, tonitrum, *thunder.*

c) In *ia*, gen. *iæ*, and *ies*, gen. *iei*:

Barbaria, barbaries, *barbarity.* Materia, materies, *matter.*

Duritia, durities, *hardness.* Mollitia, mollities, *effeminacy.*

Luxuria, luxuries, *profusion.*

d) The following:

Alimonia, *æ*, alimonium, *i, nourishment.* Buccina, *æ*, buccinum, *i, a trumpet.*

Cingulum, *i*, cingula, *æ*, a band, sash.

Consortio, *onis*, consortium, *i*, a community.

Essedium, *i*, esseda, *æ*, a war chariot.

Delphinus, *i*, delphin, *inis*, a dolphin.

Elephantus, *i*, elephas, *antis*, an elephant.

Juventus, *utis*, juventa, *æ*, and juventas, *atis* (*a* long) (personified), youth.

Mendum, *i*, menda, *æ*, a fault.

Palumbes, *is*, palumbus, *i*, and palumba, *the dove.*

Paupertas, *atis* (*a* long); (poet.) pauperies, *ei*, poverty.

Pavo, *onis* (*o* long), pavus, *i*, a peacock.

Penum, *i*, penus, *us*, and penus, *oris* (*o* short), victuals.

Plebs, *is*, plebes, *ei* (*e* short), the populace.

Senectus, *utis* (*u* long) (poet.), senecta, *æ*, old age.

Tapete, *is*, tapetum, *i*, and tapes, *etis* (*e* long), tapestry.

Vespera, *æ*, vesper (in the accusative only *vesperum*; abl. *vespere* and *vesperi*), evening; but Vesper, *i*, the evening star, is regular.

SIXTH DIVISION.

The gender of Latin nouns is ascertained

1. By the meaning,
2. By the ending.

As to the meaning, we may establish the following rules.

I. MASCULINE are: 1. All substantives representing male individuals. Ex.: *consul*, a consul; *dæmon*, a (familiar) spirit; *Deus*, God; *flamen*, a flamen (priest of Jupiter); *manes*, the manes; *pater*, a father; *scriba*, a scribe.

The following are exceptions to this rule:

a) Feminine nouns: *copiæ*, troops; *deliciæ*, a favourite; *operæ*, workmen; *vigiliæ* and *excubiæ*, sentinels.

b) Neuter nouns: *Acroama*, a buffoon; *auxilia*, auxiliary troops; *mancipium*, a slave; *servitia*, servants.

2. The names of nations, rivers, winds, months, and mountains. Ex.: *Aprilis*, April; *aquilo*, the north wind; *auster*, the south wind; *Athos*, Mount Athos; *boreas*, the north wind; *Etesiæ*, the Etesian wind; *Euphrates*, the Euphrates; *fluvius*, a river; *Hadria*, the Adriatic; *Ister*, the Danube; *notus*, the south wind; *November*, November.

The exceptions to this rule are:

a) Names of rivers: *Albula*, the Tiber; *Allia*, Rio di Mosso; *Duria*, the Doire; *Matrona*, the Marne, and the mythological rivers *Styx* and *Lethe*, which are feminine.

b) Names of mountains: *Œta*, *Peloris*, *Rhodope*, which are feminine; *Soracte* and *Pelion* are neuter.

II. FEMININE are: 1. All nouns belonging to a feminine being. Ex.: *dea*, a goddess; *filia*, a daughter;

G

lupa, a she-wolf; *mater,* a mother; *mulier,* a woman; *soror,* a sister; *uxor,* a wife.

2. The names of countries, islands, towns, precious stones, trees, and plants. Ex.: *abies,* the fir; *Ægyptus,* Egypt; *arbor,* a tree; *Carthago,* Carthage; *Corinthus,* Corinth; *Delos,* Delos; *Gallia,* Gaul; *insula,* an island; *Lacedæmon,* Sparta; *papyrus,* the papyrus; *Persis,* Persia; *pirus,* a pear-tree; *quercus,* an oak; *Rhodus,* Rhodes; *Roma,* Rome; *Salamis,* Salamis; · *Sicilia,* Sicily; *terra,* the earth; *urbs,* a city.

The exceptions to this rule are:

1. Names of countries.

A. Masculine: *Bosphorus; Isthmus,* the Isthmus of Corinth; *Hellespontus,* the Hellespont; *Pontus,* Pontus (the sea).

B. Neuter: nouns in *um,* and plurals in *a.*

Ex.: *Latium; Bactra, orum,* Bactra.

2. Names of islands. Neuter nouns in *um,* as *Dianium,* and the Greek name *Delta,* the Delta of the Nile.

3. Names of towns.

A. Masculine:

a) Names in *us,* gen. *untis.* Ex.: *Amathus,* Amathonti; *Selinus,* Selinonte; amongst those in *us,* gen. *i: Canopus,* a town in Egypt; sometimes also *Pharsalus,* Pharsalia, and *Abydus.*

b) Plural names in *i.* Ex.: *Veji,* Veiei; *Delphi.*

c) Some names in *o* and *on: Croton; Narbo* (Martius), Narbonne; *Brauron.*

d) *Tunes,* gen. *etis,* Tunis; *Taras,* gen. *antis,* Tarentum.

B. Neuter:

a) Names in *um.* Ex.: *Ilium,* Troy; *Tarentum.*

b) Names in *a,* gen. *arum.* Ex.: *Arbela; Hieroso-
lyma,* Jerusalem.

c) Names in *e* (but only in the nom. and acc.). Ex.:
Cœre, Præneste; in *ur: Tibur,* Tivoli, and also *Argos.*

d) Undeclinable or barbarous names in *i, l, r, t*:
Ex.: *Hispal, Nepet.*

4. Names of precious stones. Masculine: *beryllus,*
the beryl; *carbunculus,* the carbuncle; *opalus,* the
opal; *smaragdus,* the emerald.

5. Names of trees and shrubs.

a) Masculine:

Acanthus, *bear's-foot.*	Intubus, *chicory.*
Asparagus, *asparagus.*	Juncus, *the osier.*
Asphodelus, *asphodel.*	Oleaster, *the wild olive-tree.*
Calamus, *a reed.*	Pinaster, *the wild pine.*
Carduus, *a thistle.*	Populus, *the poplar.*
Dumus, *a bush, thicket.*	Rhamnus, *the buckthorn.*
Helleborus, *hellebore.*	Scirpus, *a bull-rush.*

Obs. Sentis, the wild rose-tree, and *vepres,* the
thorn, generally masculine, follow sometimes the
usual rule.

b) Sometimes masculine, sometimes feminine:

Amaracus, *marjoram.*	Raphanus, *horse-radish.*
Cytisus, *the cytisus.*	Rubus, *the mulberry-tree.*
Lapathus, *sorrel.*	Spinus, *the sloe.*

c) Neuter :' 1. All the names of plants in *um*. Ex.: *balsamum*, balsam.

2. The following names in *er*, gen. *eris* :

Acer, *the maple.*	Siser, *chervis.*
Cicer, *the chick-pea.*	Suber, *the cork-tree.*
Papaver, *the poppy.*	Tuber, *the truffle.*
Piper, *pepper.*	Zingiber, *ginger.*
Siler, *the osier.*	

3. *Robur*, the green oak, and *tus*, incense.

III. NEUTER are: 1. All nouns indeclinable in the singular or plural. Ex.:

Cornu, *a horn.*	Sinapi, *mustard.*
Fas, *right, justice.*	Pondo, *a pound.*
Gummi, *gum.*	Tempe, *the valley of Tempe.*
Nefas, *evil.*	

2. The names of the letters of the alphabet.

3. All words and groups of words employed as substantives. Ex.: *scire tuum*, thy knowledge; *ultimum vale*, the last farewell.

IV. The following substantives are of two genders, sometimes masculine, sometimes feminine, according as they designate a man or a woman :

Adolescens, *a youth* or *a girl.*	Artifex, *an artisan.*
Antistes, *a priest* or *priest-ess.*	Auctor, *an author, author-ess.*
	Augur, *an augur.*
Affinis, *a male* or *female relation.*	Civis, *a citizen.*
	Comes, *a companion.*

Conjux, *a husband, a wife.*
Custos, *a guardian.*
Dux, *a chief.*
Exsul, *an exile.*
Heres, *an heir, heiress.*
Hostis, *an enemy.*
Hospes, *an host, hostess.*
Incola, *an inhabitant.*
Index, *an accuser.*
Infans, *a child.*
Interpres, *an interpreter.*
Judex, *a judge.*
Juvenis, *a youth, a girl.*
Martyr, *a martyr.*

Miles, *a soldier.*
Municeps, *a freeman.*
Obses, *an hostage.*
Par, *an equal.*
Parens, *a male* or *female relation.*
Patruelis, *a cousin.*
Præsul, *a chief.*
Sacerdos, *a priest, priestess.*
Satelles, *a satellite.*
Testis, *a witness.*
Vates, *a diviner.*
Vindex, *an avenger.*

The names of the following animals have also both genders:

Anguis, *a serpent.*
Anser, *a goose.*
Bos, *an ox.*
Canis, *a dog.*
Dama, *a doe.*
Elephantus, *an elephant.*
Grus, *a stork.*
Lepus, *a hare.*

Limax, *a snail.*
Mus, *a mouse.*
Perdix, *a partridge.*
Serpens, *a serpent.*
Sus, *a hog.*
Talpa, *a mole.*
Thynnus, *a tunny-fish.*
Vespertilio, *a bat.*

V. Substantives having the same root have a distinct ending for each gender. Masculine nouns in *tor* have for the feminine *trix:* those in *us, er,* or any other ending for the masculine, have the feminine in *a.*

G 3

Avus, *a grandfather.*	Avia, *a grandmother.*
Caupo, *a landlord.*	Copa, *a landlady.*
Coquus, *a man cook.*	Coqua, *a woman-cook.*
Inventor, *an inventor.*	Inventrix, *an inventress.*
Leno, *a pander, pimp.*	Lena, *a pimp.*
Magister, *a master.*	Magistra, *a mistress.*
Præceptor, *a tutor.*	Præceptrix, *a governess.*
Puer, *a boy.*	Puella, *a girl.*
Rex, *a king.*	Regina, *a queen.*
Tibicen, *a flute-player.*	Tibicina, *a female piper.*
Ultor, *an avenger.*	Ultrix, *an avenger.*
Victor, *a conqueror.*	Victrix, *a conqueress, sub-* *duer.*

Some names of animals follow the same rule:

Agnus, *a lamb.*	Agna, *a young ewe.*
Cervus, *a stag.*	Cerva, *a doe.*
Caper, *a ram.*	Capra, *a she-goat.*
Equus, *a horse.*	Equa, *a mare.*
Gallus, *a cock.*	Gallina, *a hen.*
Juvencus, *a young bull.*	Juvenca, *a heifer.*
Lupus, *a wolf.*	Lupa, *a she-wolf.*
Leo, *a lion.*	Lea or Leæna, *a lioness.*
Ursus, *a bear.*	Ursa, *a she-bear.*
Vitulus, *a calf.*	Vitula, *a heifer.*
Taurus, *a bull.*	Vacca, *a cow.*
Aries, *a ram.*	Ovis, *a sheep.*
Hædus, *a he-goat.*	Capella, *a she-goat.*

Obs. A. The nouns *coluber* and *colubra,* a snake;
lacertus and *lacerta,* a lizard; *luscinius* and *luscinia,* a
nightingale; *simius* and *simia,* a monkey, are used

either male or female; and the feminine form is more generally employed to mark both genders; we must not therefore suppose that *simia* means a female ape.

Obs. B. Most other names of animals have one gender only, viz. their grammatical gender according to their ending. If we wish to indicate a male or a female, we add the words *mas*, male, and *femina*, female.

<hr />

GENDER OF LATIN SUBSTANTIVES ACCORDING TO THEIR TERMINATION.

1. MASCULINE are: nouns ending in the nominative case with *us, er, o, or, os, es* (imparisyllabic), and the Greek nouns in *as, es, an, en, in, on.* Ex.:

Dominus, *a lord or master.*
Puer, *a boy.*
Homo, *a man.*

Error, *error.*
Nepos, *a grandson.*
Miles, *a soldier.*

EXCEPTION I.—NOUNS IN *us.*

1. FEMININE.

1. Feminine nouns in *us*, gen. *i.*

a) On account of their signification, the names of towns, of islands, trees, and plants, in *us.* (See p. 74, substantives of this class that remain masculine.)

b) The following substantives: *alvus*, the stomach;

carbasus, linen cloth; *colus,* a distaff; *humus,* the ground; *vannus,* a fan.

c) The following nouns, derived from the Greek, and retaining the gender to which they belong in that language:

Abyssus, *an abyss.*	Diphthongus, *a diphthong.*
Antidotus, *an antidote.*	Epodus, *an epod.*
Arctus, *the bear* (constellation).	Eremus, *a desert.*
	Exodus, *an exit.*
Atomus, *an atom.*	Methodus, *method.*
Apostrophus, *an apostrophe.*	Paragraphus, *a paragraph.*
	Perimetrus, *the perimeter.*
Cathetus, *the catheter.*	Periodus, *a period.*
Dialectus, *a dialect.*	Synodus, *a synod.*
Diametrus, *the diameter.*	

2. Feminine nouns in *us,* gen. *us.*

a) By their signification:

Anus, *an old woman.*	Quercus, *an oak.*
Ficus, *a fig-tree.*	Socrus, *a mother-in-law.*
Nurus, *a daughter-in-law.*	

b) The following:

Acus, *a needle.*	Manus, *the hand.*
Domus, *a house.*	Porticus, *a portico.*
Idus (no sing., gen.*Iduum*), *the Ides* (*of the month*).	Tribus, *a tribe.*

3. Feminine nouns in *us,* gen. *utis* (see p. 29):

Juventus, *youth.*	Servitus, *slavery.*
Salus, *safety.*	Virtus, *virtue.*
Senectus, *old age.*	

And the following:

Incus (gen. *incudis*), *an anvil.*

Intercus (gen. *intercutis*), *the dropsy.*

Palus (gen. *paludis*), *a marsh.*

Pecus (gen. *pecudis*), *cattle.*

Tellus (gen. *telluris*), *the earth.*

Venus (gen. *Veneris*), *Venus.*

2. NEUTER.

1. Neuter nouns in *us*, gen. *i*:

Vulgus, *the populace.*

Pelagus, *the sea.*

Virus, *venom.*

2. Neuter nouns in *us*, gen. *oris* (see p. 36):

Dedecus, *dishonour.*

Facinus, *a (foul) deed.*

Fenus, *usury.*

Frigus, *cold.*

Pectus, *the chest.*

Pecus, *cattle.*

Pignus, *a pledge.*

Stercus, *filth.*

Tempus, *time.*

Obs. Lepus, gen. *leporis,* a hare, is masculine and feminine.

3. Neuter nouns in *us*, gen. *eris* (see p. 36):

Fœdus, *an alliance.*

Funus, *a funeral.*

Latus, *the side.*

Olus, *vegetables.*

Opus, *a work.*

Pondus, *a weight.*

Scelus, *crime.*

Sidus, *a star.*

Ulcus, *an ulcer.*

4. Neuter nouns in *us*, gen. *uris:*

Crus (gen. *cruris*), *the leg.*

Jus, *law.*

Pus, *matter.*

Rus, *the country.*

Thus, *incense.*

Obs. For *mus*, gen. *muris*, a mouse; *grus*, gen. *gruis*, a stork; *sus*, gen. *suis*, a hog, see p. 38. 53, 54.

EXCEPTION II.—NOUNS IN *o*.

FEMININE.

a) Most nouns ending in *do*, *go*, *io*, except *cupido*, desire, and the nouns mentioned, p. 56, as examples and exceptions, which are masculine.

b) *Caro*, gen. *carnis*, flesh; *echo*, echo (p. 44); *Argo*.

EXCEPTION III.—NOUNS IN *or*.

1. FEMININE.

One only, *arbor*, gen. *oris*, a tree [1].

2. NEUTER.

The four following: *ador*, flour of wheat; *æquor*, gen. *oris*, the surface, the sea; *cor*, gen. *cordis*, the heart; *marmor*, gen. *oris*, marble.

EXCEPTION IV.—NOUNS IN *os*.

1. FEMININE.

Cos (gen. *cotis*), *a grinding-stone.*

Eos (gen. *eus*), *the dawn.*

Dos (gen. *dotis*), *a dower.*

Glos (gen. *gloris*), *a sister-in-law.*

---

[1] Of course we do not mention those which are feminine by their signification, as *soror*, a sister, *uxor*, a wife (see the gender of substantives determined by their signification, p. 74).

2. NEUTER.

Os (*oris*), *the mouth.*	Ethos, *custom.*
Os (*ossis*), *a bone.*	Epos, *an epic poem.*
Chaos.	Melos, *a song.*

EXCEPTION V.—NOUNS IN *er* (gen. *is*).

1. FEMININE.

a) Mater, a mother.

b) Linter, a skiff (often also masculine).

2. NEUTER.

a) The names of plants :

Acer, *the maple.*	Siler, *the osier.*
Cicer, *the chick-pea.*	Siser, *the parsnip.*
Papaver, *the poppy.*	Suber, *cork.*
Piper, *pepper.*	Zingiber, *ginger.*

b) The following substantives :

Cadaver, *a corpse.*	Uber, *the breast.*
Iter, *a road.*	Ver, *spring.*
Spinther or Spinter, *a bracelet.*	Verbera, *blows* (plur. of an obsolete sing. *verber*).
Tuber, *a tumor.*	

EXCEPTION VI.—NOUNS IN *es* (imparisyllabic).

1. FEMININE.

Compedes (plur.), *fetters.*	pounds : *requies,* repose ;
Merces, *a reward.*	and *inquies,* anxiety.
Merges, *a sheaf.*	Seges, *harvest.*
Quies, *rest,* and its com-	Teges, *an osier-mat.*

2. NEUTER.

The only one is *æs* (gen. *æris*), brass.

EXCEPTION VII.—NOUNS IN *ex*.

FEMININE.

a) The names of trees and plants:

Atriplex, *the orach* (also neuter).
Carex, *sedge*.

Ilex, *the scarlet oak.*
Vitex, *agnus castus.*

b) The following:

Fæx, *dregs.*
Forpices, *a pair of pincers* (from the sing. *forpex*, but little used).
Lex, *law.*

Nex, *(violent) death.*
Preces, *prayers* (from the obsolete sing. *prex*).
Supellex, *household furniture.*

II. FEMININE are: substantives ending in *a* (gen. *æ*), *as, is, es* (parisyllabic), *ys, s* preceded by a consonant, *x* (except nouns in *ex*), *do, go, io,* and two words in *aus—fraus,* fraud, and *laus,* praise. Nouns in *es,* gen. *ei,* of which we have given the principal examples, p. 27, as well as Greek substantives in *e* (see p. 44), are also feminine. Ex.:

Mensa, *a table.*
Ætas, *an age.*
Navis, *a ship.*
Nubes, *a cloud.*

Pars, *a part.*
Pax, *peace.*
Res, *a thing.*
Epitome, *an abridgement.*

EXCEPTION I.—NOUNS IN *a*.

1. MASCULINE.

According to their signification. The following are those most in use :

Advena, *a stranger.*
Agricola, *a labourer.*
Assecla, *a follower.*
Bibliopola, *a bookseller.*
Collega, *a colleague.*
Homicida, *a murderer.*
Nauta, *a sailor.*

Parricida, *a parricide.*
Perfuga, *a deserter.*
Pirata, *a pirate.*
Poeta, *a poet.*
Scriba, *a scribe.*
Scurra, *a buffoon.*
Transfuga, *a deserter.*

2. NEUTER.

All nouns in *ma*, gen. *matis.* Ex.: *poema*, a poem.

EXCEPTION II.—NOUNS IN *as*.

1. MASCULINE.

a) Greek nouns in *as*, gen. *antis* : *adamas*, the dia-mond; *elephas*, an elephant; and the names of mountains: *Acragas, Atlas, Mimas.*

b) The following substantives : *as* (gen. *assis*), a Roman penny; *mas* (gen. *maris*), a male; *vas* (gen. *vadis*), a surety (bail).

2. NEUTER.

a) *Vas* (gen. *vasis*), a vase. *b)* The indeclinable nouns, *fas*, what is lawful, and *nefas*, what is un-

H

lawful. *c*) Greek nouns in *as*, gen. *atis*, as *arto-creas*, a pie.

EXCEPTION III.—NOUNS IN *is*.

MASCULINE.

a) The following nouns:

Amnis, *a river.*
Axis, *an axis.*
Callis, *a pathway.*
Canalis, *a canal.*
Cassis (gen. used in the plur. *casses*), *a net.*
Caulis *or* colis, *a stalk.*
Cinis (gen. *eris*), *ashes.*
Collis, *a hill.*
Crinis, *the hair.*
Cucumis (gen. *eris*), *the cucumber.*
Ensis, *a sword.*
Fascis (gener. used in the plur.), *the fasces.*
Finis, *the end.*
Follis, *a pair of bellows.*
Funis, *a rope.*
Fustis, *a stick.*

Glis (g. *gliris*), *a dormouse.*
Ignis, *fire.*
Lapis (gen. *lapidis*), *stone.*
Mensis, *a month.*
Orbis, *a circle.*
Panis, *bread.*
Piscis, *a fish.*
Postis, *a post.*
Pulvis (gen. *eris*), *dust.*
Sanguis (gen. *inis*), *blood.*
Scrobis, *a ditch, a furrow.*
Sentis, *a briar.*
Torquis, *a necklace.*
Torris, *a firebrand.*
Unguis, *a nail* (claw).
Vectis, *a lever.*
Vermis, *a worm.*
Vomis (gen. *eris*), *a plough-share.*

b) The following, originally adjectives and referring to a masculine substantive understood:

Annalis (generally used in the plur. *annales*, *libri* understood), *annals.*

Jugales (*equi*), *a team,* or *yoke, of horses.*
Molaris (*lapis*), *a mill-*

stone, or (if *dens* is understood) *a molar tooth.*

Natalis (*dies*), *a birthday.*
Pugillares (*libelli*), *tablets.*

c) According to their signification, the names of months: *Aprilis,* April; *Quintilis,* July; *Sextilis,* August.

EXCEPTION IV.—NOUNS IN *es* (parisyllabic).

MASCULINE.

Acinaces, *a scymitar.*
Palumbes, *a pigeon.*

Vepres (no sing.), *the thorn.*

N.B. The two last substantives are also employed in the feminine.

EXCEPTION V.—NOUNS IN *s* (preceded by a consonant).

MASCULINE.

a) The following substantives:

Adeps, *fat.*
Dens, *a tooth.*
Fons, *a fountain.*

Mons, *a mountain.*
Pons, *a bridge.*

b) The following substantives, originally adjectives or participles, referring to a masculine substantive understood:

Bidens (*raster*), *a hoe* [1].
Confluens (generally used in the plur. *confluentes,*

amnes understood), *a flowing together, conflux.*
Dodrans, *nine ounces.*

---

[1] *Bidens* is feminine when it means an ewe of two years old.

Oriens et occidens (*sol* understood), *the east and west.*

Quadrans, *three ounces.*

Rudens (*funis*), *a cable.*

Sextans, *two ounces.*

Tridens (*raster*), *a trident.*

Triens, *four ounces* (*as* understood).

Torrens (*amnis*), *a torrent.*

c) Greek substantives:

Chalybs, *steel.*

Ellops (gen. *opis*), *the sturgeon.*

Gryps (gen. *gryphis*), *a griffin.*

Hydrops, *a dropsical person.*

Obs. Serpens, a serpent, is masculine in poetry; *stirps*, the trunk of a tree, is masculine, but feminine when it means a race, issue; *seps*, a serpent, and *continens*, a continent, are sometimes masculine, sometimes feminine.

EXCEPTION VI.—NOUNS IN *x*.

MASCULINE.

a) Nouns in *ax*: Greek nouns with this ending. Except: *climax*, a ladder, which is feminine.

b) In *ix*: *calix*, a chalice, cup; *fornix*, a vault; *phœnix*, the phœnix; *sorix* or *saurix*, the name of a bird; *varix*, a varicose vein.

c) In *yx*: the following Greek nouns:

Calyx, *the centre of a flower.*

Coccyx (gen. *coccygis*), *a cuckoo.*

Onyx (gen. *onychis*), *onyx.*

Bombyx, *the silk-worm.*

d) In *ux*: *tradux* (*palmes* understood), a grafted branch.

EXCEPTION VII.—NOUNS IN *do*.

MASCULINE.

Cardo, *a hinge.*	Ordo, *order.*
Cudo, *a helmet.*	Prædo (*onis*), *a brigand.*
Cupido, *Cupid* (in poetry).	Spado (*onis*), *an eunuch.*
Mango (*onis*), *a slave-dealer.*	Udo, *a sock.*

EXCEPTION VIII.—NOUNS IN *go*.

MASCULINE.

Harpago, a harpoon; *ligo*, a hoe; *margo*, the margin.

EXCEPTION IX.—NOUNS IN *io*.

MASCULINE.

a) The following nouns:

Cucullio, *a hood.*	Scopio, *a bunch of grapes.*
Matellio, *an ewer.*	Septentrio, *the north.*
Unio, *a pearl.*	Titio, *a firebrand.*
Pugio, *a dagger.*	Turio, *a shoot* (of plants).
Scipio, *a staff.*	

b) Numbers: *ternio*, the figure three; *quaternio*, the figure four, &c.

c) Many names of animals. Ex.:

Curculio, *a weevil.*	Stellio, *a lizard.*
Papilio, *a butterfly.*	Vespertilio, *a bat.*
Scorpio, *a scorpion.*	

EXCEPTION X.—NOUNS IN *es* (gen. *ei*).

MASCULINE.

Dies, day, and *meridies*, noon.

Obs. *Dies* is feminine when it means a space of time, a whole day or a particular day.

III. NEUTER are substantives ending in *um, u, e* (gen. *is*), *l, en, ar, ur;* Greek nouns ending in *ma, i, y;* and the two words ending in *c : alec* or *halec,* gen. *halecis,* a herring, and *lac,* gen. *lactis,* milk : as well as the only noun ending in *t : caput,* gen. *capitis,* the head, and its compounds *occiput,* gen. *occipitis,* the back of the head, and *sinciput,* the front of the head.   Ex. :

Bellum, *war.*	Nomen, *a name.*
Cornu, *a horn.*	Calcar, *a spur.*
Mare, *the sea.*	Fulgur, *lightning.*
Animal, *an animal.*	

EXCEPTIONS.

MASCULINE.

NOUNS IN *l.*

Consul, *a consul.*	Pugil, *an athlete.*
Exul, *an exile.*	Sal, *salt.*
Mugil, *the mullet.*	Sol, *the sun.*
Præsul, *the first of the Sabines.*	

NOUNS IN *ar.*

Par, an even number, is both masculine and feminine.   But *par*, a pair, follows the general rule.

NOUNS IN *ur.*

Fur, *a thief.*	Turtur, *a dove.*
Furfur, *a sound.*	Vultur, *a vulture.*

NOUNS IN *en.*

Attagen, *the heath-cock.*	Pecten (*inis*), *a comb.*
Lichen, *the lichen.*	Ren, *the back.*
Lien, *the milt.*	Splen, *spleen.*

Also, on account of their meaning, *fidicen*, a performer on the lyre; *tibicen*, a performer on the flute, and others ending in *cen*.

CHAPTER II.

DECLENSION OF ADJECTIVES.

THE Latin adjective agrees in number, gender, and case, with the substantive of which it is the epithet or attribute.

The adjective has therefore three genders, and agrees in gender with the substantive which it accompanies. As however the different genders are not always expressed by a particular termination, adjectives are divided into three classes.

1. Adjectives having three terminations, i. e., having a termination peculiar to each of the three genders.

2. Adjectives having only two terminations, one for the masculine and feminine, and another for the neuter.

3. Adjectives having in the singular but one termination for the three genders.

FIRST CLASS.

Adjectives having three terminations.

The adjectives having three terminations are:

a) Those in *us* masculine, *a* feminine, *um* neuter. Ex.: *Bonus, bona, bonum,* good.

b) Those in *er* masculine, *(r)a* feminine, *(r)um* neuter. Ex.: *Pulcher, pulchra, pulchrum,* handsome; one only ending in *ur : satur, satura, saturum,* satisfied (satiated).

I. TABLE

OF THE DECLENSION OF ADJECTIVES HAVING THREE TERMINATIONS.

	Singular.			*Plural.*		
	Masc.	Fem.	Neuter.	Mas.	Fem.	Neuter.
N.	us (*er*)	a	um	N. i	æ	a
G.	i	æ	i	G. orum	arum	orum
D.	o	æ	o	D. is, for the three genders.		
A.	um	am	um	A. os	as	a
V.	e (*er*)	a	um	V. i	æ	a
A.	o	a	o	A. is, for the three genders.		

By this table we see that the masculine is declined like the nouns in *us,* gen. *i* (or *er,* gen. *i*), the feminine like the feminine in *a,* and the neuter like neuter nouns in *um.*

Obs. Adjectives ending in *er, a, um,* generally reject the *e* of the ending, as we have seen in *pulcher,* above.

The following adjectives are those only that retain the *e*.

Asper, *rugged, sour.*	Liber, *free.*
Exter, *external.*	Miser, *miserable.*
Gibber, *humpbacked.*	Prosper, *prosperous.*
Lacer, *torn.*	Tener, *tender.*

Also the adjectives derived from the verbs *fero*
and *gero* (to bear). Ex.: *Mortifer*, deadly; *aliger*,
winged; *frugifer*, fruitful.

EXAMPLES.

*Adjectives having three terminations declined with a
substantive.*

 a) Adjectives in *us, a, um.*

1. MASCULINE.

Singular.	*Plural.*
N. Pater bonus, *a good father.*	N. Patres boni, *good fathers.*
G. Patris boni, *of a good father.*	G. Patrum bonorum, *of good fathers.*
D. Patri bono, *to a good father.*	D. Patribus bonis, *to good fathers.*
A. Patrem bonum, *a good father.*	A. Patres bonos, *good fathers.*
V. ô Pater bone, *o good father.*	V. ô Patres boni, *o good fathers.*
A. Patre bono, *from or by a good father.*	A. Patribus bonis, *from or by good fathers.*

2. Feminine.

Singular.	*Plural.*
N. Urbs opulenta, *a rich city.*	N. Urbes opulentæ, *rich cities.*
G. Urbis opulentæ, *of a rich city.*	G. Urbium opulentarum, *of rich cities.*
D. Urbi opulentæ, *to a rich city.*	D. Urbibus opulentis, *to rich cities.*
A. Urbem opulentam, *a rich city.*	A. Urbes opulentas, *rich cities.*
V. ô Urbs opulenta, *o rich city.*	V. ô Urbes opulentæ, *o rich cities.*
A. Urbe opulenta, *from* or *by a rich city.*	A. Urbibus opulentis, *from* or *by rich cities.*

3. NEUTER.

N. Egregium facinus, *a noble action.*	N. Egregia facinora, *noble actions.*
G. Egregii facinoris, *of a noble action.*	G. Egregiorum facinorum, *of noble actions.*
D. Egregio facinori, *to a noble action.*	D. Egregiis facinoribus, *to noble actions.*
A. Egregium facinus, *a noble action.*	A. Egregia facinora, *noble actions.*
V. ô Egregium facinus, *o noble action.*	V. ô Egregia facinora, *o noble actions.*
A. Egregio facinore, *from* or *by a noble action.*	A. Egregiis facinoribus, *from* or *by noble actions.*

96 DECLENSION OF ADJECTIVES.

b) Adjectives in *er, a, um*.

1. MASCULINE.

Singular.	*Plural.*
N. Homo liber, *a free man.*	N. Homines liberi, *free men.*
G. Hominis liberi, *of a free man.*	G. Hominum liberorum, *of free men.*
D. Homini libero, *to a free man.*	D. Hominibus liberis, *to free men.*
A. Hominem liberum, *a free man.*	A. Homines liberos, *free men.*
V. ô Homo liber, *o free man.*	V. ô Homines liberi, *o free men.*
A. Homine libero, *from or by a free man.*	A. Hominibus liberis, *from or by free men.*

2. FEMININE.

N. Terra frugifera, *a fruitful land.*	N. Terræ frugiferæ, *fruitful lands.*
G. Terræ frugiferæ, *of a fruitful land.*	G. Terrarum frugiferarum, *of fruitful lands.*
D. Terræ frugiferæ, *to a fruitful land.*	D. Terris frugiferis, *to fruitful lands.*
A. Terram frugiferam, *a fruitful land.*	A. Terras frugiferas, *fruitful lands.*
V. ô Terra frugifera, *o fruitful land.*	V. ô Terræ frugiferæ, *o fruitful lands.*
A. Terra frugifera, *from or by a fruitful land.*	A. Terris frugiferis, *from or by fruitful lands.*

NEUTER.

N. Pulchrum cubile, *a fine room.*

N. Pulchra cubilia, *fine rooms.*

G. Pulchri cubilis, *of a fine room.*

G. Pulchrorum cubilium, *of fine rooms.*

D. Pulchro cubili, *to a fine room.*

D. Pulchris cubilibus, *to fine rooms.*

A. Pulchrum cubile, *a fine room.*

A. Pulchra cubilia, *fine rooms.*

V. ô Pulchrum cubile, *o fine room.*

V. ô Pulchra cubilia, *o fine rooms.*

A. Pulchro cubili, *from or by a fine room.*

A. Pulchris cubilibus, *from or by fine rooms.*

Obs. The pupil can easily select similar examples of substantives in the lists of the first chapter on the declension of nouns and of adjectives in the Method or the Dictionary.

SECOND CLASS.

Adjectives having only two Terminations for the three Genders.

These adjectives have the ending *is* for the masculine and feminine, and *e* for the neuter.

I

II. TABLE

OF THE DECLENSION OF ADJECTIVES HAVING ONLY
TWO TERMINATIONS FOR THE THREE GENDERS.

Singular.		*Plural.*	
Masc. and Fem.	**Neuter.**	**Masc. and Fem.**	**Neuter.**
N. is	e	N. es	ia
G. is for the three gen-		G. ium for the three	
	ders.		genders.
D. i	*id.*	D. ibus	*id.*
A. em	e	A. es	ia
V. is	e	V. es	ia
A. i for the three genders.		A. ibus for the three	
			genders.

EXAMPLES

Of Adjectives having only two Terminations, declined
with a Noun.

1. MASCULINE.

Singular.	*Plural.*
N. Fidel*is* amic*us, a faith-* *ful friend.*	N. Fidel*es* amic*i, faithful* *friends.*
G. Fidel*is* amic*i, of a faith-* *ful friend.*	G. Fidel*ium* amic*orum, of* *faithful friends.*
D. Fidel*i* amic*o, to a faith-* *ful friend.*	D. Fidel*ibus* amic*is, to* *faithful friends.*
A. Fidel*em* amic*um, a* *faithful friend.*	A. Fidel*es* amic*os, faith-* *ful friends.*

V. ô Fidelis amice, *o faith-* | V. ô Fideles amici, *o faith-*
ful friend. | *ful friends.*
A. Fideli amico, *from* or | A. Fidelibus amicis, *from*
by a faithful friend. | or *by faithful friends.*

2. FEMININE.

N. Dulcis uva, *a sweet* | N. Dulces uvæ, *sweet*
grape. | *grapes.*
G. Dulcis uvæ, *of a sweet* | G. Dulcium uvarum, *of*
grape. | *sweet grapes.*
D. Dulci uvæ, *to a sweet* | D. Dulcibus uvis, *to sweet*
grape. | *grapes.*
A. Dulcem uvam, *a sweet* | A. Dulces uvas, *sweet*
grape. | *grapes.*
V. ô Dulcis uva, *o sweet* | V. ô Dulces uvæ, *o sweet*
grape. | *grapes.*
A. Dulci uva, *from* or *by* | A. Dulcibus uvis, *from* or
a sweet grape. | *by sweet grapes.*

3. NEUTER.

N. Bellum crudele, *cruel* | N. Bella crudelia, *cruel*
war. | *wars.*
G. Belli crudelis, *of cruel* | G. Bellorum crudelium, *of*
war. | *cruel wars.*
D. Bello crudeli, *to cruel* | D. Bellis crudelibus, *to*
war. | *cruel wars.*
A. Bellum crudele, *cruel* | A. Bella crudelia, *cruel*
war. | *wars.*
V. ô Bellum crudele, *o* | V. ô Bella crudelia, *o cruel*
cruel war. | *wars.*
A. Bello crudeli, *from* or | A. Bellis crudelibus, *from*
by cruel war. | or *by cruel wars.*

Obs. The thirteen following adjectives, although belonging to this declension, have in the nominative case a termination peculiar to the masculine in *er.* They are, as for the other cases, declined according to the above table.

Acer, acris, acre, *strong, lively.*

Alacer, alacris, alacre, *awake, ready.*

Campester, campestris, campestre, *rural.*

Celeber, celebris, celebre, *famous.*

Celer, celeris, celere, *prompt.*

Equester, equestris, equestre, *equestrian.*

Paluster, palustris, palustre, *marshy.*

Pedester, pedestris, pedestre, *pedestrian.*

Puter, putris, putre, *rotten.*

Saluber, salubris, salubre, *wholesome.*

Silvester, silvestris, silvestre, *sylvan.*

Terrester, terrestris, terrestre, *terrestrial.*

Volucer, volucris, volucre, *winged.*

Celer is the only one that for euphony retains the *e* : feminine, *celeris* (*e* short) ; neuter, *celere* (*e* short).

THIRD CLASS.

Adjectives having but one Termination in the Singular for the three Genders.

Almost all these adjectives have the nominative case in *ns ;* some in *x,* rarely in *r* or *l ;* they are

declined like the substantives having these terminations. It is to be observed only that the ablative
singular ends in *i* rather than *e*.

III. TABLE

OF THE DECLENSION OF ADJECTIVES HAVING ONLY
ONE TERMINATION FOR THE THREE GENDERS.

Singular.		*Plural.*	
Masc. and Fem.	Neuter.	Masc. and Fem.	Neuter.
N. undetermined.		N. es	ia
G. is for the three genders.		G. ium *or* um for the three genders.	
D. i	*id.*	D. ibus	*id.*
A. em (the neuter like the nominative).		A. like the nominative.	
V. like the nominative.		V. *id.*	*id.*
A. i *or* e for the three genders.		A. ibus for the three genders.	

EXAMPLE

OF ADJECTIVES WITH ONLY ONE TERMINATION DECLINED WITH A SUBSTANTIVE.

Singular.

N. Felix miles, a happy soldier.
G. Felicis militis, of a happy soldier.
D. Felici militi, to a happy soldier.
A. Felicem militem, a happy soldier.
V. ô Felix miles, o happy soldier.
A. Felici milite, from or by a happy soldier.

N. Felix mater, a happy mother.
G. Felicis matris, of a happy mother.
D. Felici matri, to a happy mother.
A. Felicem matrem, a happy mother.
V. ô Felix mater, o happy mother.
A. Felici matre, from or by a happy mother.

N. Felix miraculum, a fortunate miracle.
G. Felicis miraculi, of a fortunate miracle.
D. Felici miraculo, to a fortunate miracle.
A. Felix miraculum, a fortunate miracle.
V. ô Felix miraculum, o fortunate miracle.
A. Felici miraculo, from or by a fortunate miracle.

Plural.

N. Felices milites, happy soldiers.
G. Felicium militum, of happy soldiers.
D. Felicibus militibus, to happy soldiers.
A. Felices milites, happy soldiers.
V. ô Felices milites, o happy soldiers.
A. Felicibus militibus, from or by happy soldiers.

N. Felices matres, happy mothers.
G. Felicium matrum, of happy mothers.
D. Felicibus matribus, to happy mothers.
A. Felices matres, happy mothers.
V. ô Felices matres, o happy mothers.
A. Felicibus matribus, from or by happy mothers.

N. Felicia miracula, fortunate miracles.
G. Felicium miraculorum, of fortunate miracles.
D. Felicibus miraculis, to fortunate miracles.
A. Felicia miracula, fortunate miracles.
V. ô Felicia miracula, o fortunate miracles.
A. Felicibus miraculis, from or by fortunate miracles.

REMARKS ON SOME CASES OF ADJECTIVES HAVING
ONLY ONE TERMINATION.

1. *Genitive Singular.*

or, gen. like the nouns. Except *memor, oris* (*o*
short).

ur, gen. *uris* (*u* short). *Cicur,* tame.

es, gen. *itis* (*i* short). *Ales* (winged), *cæres* (from
Cære), *cocles* (one-eyed), *dives* (rich), *sospes*
(safe), *superstes* (surviving).

gen. *etis* (*e* short). *Hebes* (blunted), *indiges* (indi-
gent), *præpes* (flying rapidly), *teres* (round).

gen. *etis* (*e* long). *Locuples* (rich).

gen. *idis* (*i* short). *Deses, reses* (lazy).

Pubes (having attained puberty), and *im-
pubes* (not having attained puberty),
have *eris* (*e* short).

os, gen. *otis* (*o* short). *Compos* (possessing), and
impos (unable).

us, gen. *eris* (*e* short). *Vetus* (old).

rs ⎱ gen. like the nouns. *Concors* (united), *discors*
ns ⎰ (disunited), *misericors* (merciful), derived
from *cor,* gen. *cordis,* the heart, have the
genitive *concordis, discordis, misericordis.*

bs ⎱ gen. like the substantives. *Cœlebs* (bachelor),
ps ⎰ gen. *cœlibis* (*i* short); those ending in *ceps*
have the genitive in *cipis* (*i* short). Ex. :
princeps, gen. *principis* (principal); *anceps*
(doubtful), and *præceps* (headlong), have
the gen. *ancipitis, præcipitis.*

x, gen. like the nouns; therefore

ax, gen. *acis* (*a* long); *ex*, gen. *icis*, but *exlex* (lawless), *exlegis*.

ix, gen. *icis* (*i* long); *ox*, gen. *ocis* (*o* long), but *præcox* (precocious), *præcocis* (*o* short).

2. *Ablative singular.*

This case takes *i* or *e*; but the ending in *i* is to be preferred. Some adjectives however have it exclusively in *e*; they are:

a) All those in *es*, except *hebes*, blunted, and *teres*, round.

b) The following: *compos*, *impos*, *pauper*, poor; *senex*, old; *princeps*, and *particeps*, partaking of.

c) Those which are derived from substantives having the ablative in *e*.

  Ex.: *tricolor*, having three colours.

Others have the ablative exclusively in *i*; they are:

a) Those in *x*.

b) Adjectives in *ns*, which were originally participles.

c) Those in *ceps*, gen. *cipitis*.

d) And the following:

Concors, *united.*	Inops, *poor.*
Discors, *disunited.*	Iners, *inert.*
Hebes, *blunted.*	Memor, *mindful.*
Immemor, *forgetful.*	Par, *even* (in number).
Impar, *uneven* (in number).	Recens, *recent.*
Ingens, *large.*	Repens, *sudden.*

Obs. Adjectives employed as substantives have always the ablative in *e*.

3. *Nom.* (*acc. and voc.*) *plural neuter.*

When adjectives belonging to this class are joined to a neuter substantive they take the ending *ia* in the nom. acc. and voc. cases plural; but besides those ending in *as, ns, rs, x* (except those in *fex*), there are a few which have the three cases alike in the plural neuter. Further, *dives*, rich, and *par*, equal, have *ditia* and *paria*. *Plus*, more, has *plura; vetus*, old, *vetera*. The others are not to be found in the nom. acc. and voc. plural neuter.

4. *Genitive plural.*

Have *um* instead of *ium :*

a) Those adjectives which have only *e* in the ablative singular. (See above, 2.)

b) Those ending in *ceps* and *fex.* Ex.: *princeps*, principal.

c) Those ending in *bs* and *ps.* Ex.: *inops*, poor.

d) The following :

Celer, *rapid.*	Supplex, *suppliant.*
Cicur, *tame.*	Uber, *fertile.*
Dives, *rich.*	Vetus, *old.*
Memor, *mindful.*	Vigil, *vigilant.*
Immemor, *forgetful.*	

e) Those which are derived from substantives having *um* in the genitive plural. Ex.: *tricolor.*

Indeclinable Adjectives.

Damnas, *obliged.*	Nequam, *wicked.*
Frugi, *excellent.*	Potis *or* pote, *capable.*
Necesse, *necessary.*	

A GENERAL TABLE OF THE DECLENSION OF LATIN ADJECTIVES.

1. Adjectives with three terminations.

SINGULAR.

	Masc.	Fem.	Neuter.
N.	us (er)	a	um
G.	i	æ	i
D.	o	æ	o
A.	um	am	um
V.	e (er)	a	um
A.	o	a	o

PLURAL.

	Masc.	Fem.	Neuter.
N.	i	æ	a
G.	orum	arum	orum
D.	is for the three genders.		
A.	os	as	a
V.	i	æ	a
A.	is for all three genders.		

2. Adjectives with two terminations.

SINGULAR.

	Masc. and Fem.	Neuter.
N.	is	e
G.	is } for the three genders.	
D.	i }	
A.	em	e
V.	is	e
A.	i for all three genders.	

PLURAL.

	Masc. and Fem.	Neuter.
N.	es	ia
G.	ium } for the three genders.	
D.	ibus }	
A.	es	ia
V.	es	ia
A.	ibus for all three genders.	

3. Adjectives with one termination.

	Masc.	Fem.	Neuter.
N.	.		
G.	is } for the three genders.		
D.	i }		
A.	em, neut. like the nom.		
V.	like the nominative.		
A.	i (e) for the three gend.		

ON THE COMPARATIVE AND SUPERLATIVE OF
ADJECTIVES.

A. *Formation of the Comparative and Superlative.*

1. The comparative is formed by adding to the root the ending *ior* for the masculine and feminine, and the ending *ius* for the neuter. Ex.: *carus, a, um,* dear, comparative car*ior,* neuter car*ius.*

2. The superlative is formed by adding to the root the ending *issimus* (fem. *a,* neuter *um*). Ex.: *carus,* superlative car*issimus,* car*issima,* car*issimum.*

Obs. The root is obtained by taking away the termination of the genitive. Ex.:

POSITIVE.	GEN.	RADIC.	COMPAR.	SUPERL.
clarus (a, um), *clear*	clar-i	clar-	clar-ior, ius	clarissimus, a, um
levis (e), *light*	levis	lev-	lev-ior, lev-ius	levissimus, a, um
prudens, *wise*	pru-dent-is	pru-dent-	prudent-ior, pru-dent-ius	prudentissi-mus (a, um)

EXCEPTION I.

Adjectives in *er,* instead of forming the superlative in *issimus,* add to the nominative case the ending *rimus.* Ex.: *pulcher (a, um),* handsome; compar.,

pulch*rior, ius,* superl. pulcher*rimus (a, um)*; *miser
(a, um)*, poor; compar. miser*ior, ius,* superl. miser*rimus (a, um).*

Obs. 1. *Vetus* (gen. *veteris*), old, has the same
formation; superl. veter*rimus* (compar. better *vetus-
tior,* from *vetustus,* than *veterior*).

Obs. 2. Adjectives in *er,* which have *e* in their
declension, retain it in the formation of the comparative. Ex.: *tener,* tender, gen. *teneri,* compar.
tenerior; celer, swift, gen. *celeris,* compar. *celerior.*

EXCEPTION II.

The six following adjectives in *ilis* form the superlative by adding *limus* to the root.

Facilis, *easy.*	*Sup.* Facillimus.
Difficilis, *difficult.*	Difficillimus.
Similis, *alike.*	Simillimus.
Dissimilis, *dissimilar.*	Dissimillimus.
Gracilis, *graceful.*	Gracillimus.
Humilis, *humble.*	Humillimus.

EXCEPTION III.

Adjectives in *dicus, ficus, volus,* derived from the
verbs *dico,* I say, *facio,* I do, *volo,* I will, form the
comparative and superlative with obsolete positives,
ending in *dicens, ficens, volens,* thus:

Positive.	*Comp.*	*Superl.*
Maledicus, *slande-rous.*	Maledicentior.	Maledicentissi-mus.

Positive.	Comp.	Superl.
Munificus, *gene-rous.*	Munificentior,	Munificentis-simus.
Benevolus, *bene-volent.*	Benevolentior.	Benevolentis-simus.

Egenus, needy, forms its comparative and superlative in a similar manner: *egentior, egentissimus.*

EXCEPTION IV.

The following adjectives form their comparative and superlative in an irregular manner:

Positive.	Comp.		Superl.
	Masc. and Fem.	Neuter.	
Bonus, *good.*	melior, *better.*	melius,	optimus, *best.*
Malus, *bad.*	pejor, *worse.*	pejus,	pessimus, *worst.*
Magnus, *great.*	major, *greater.*	majus,	maximus, *greatest.*
Parvus, *little.*	minor, *less.*	minus,	minimus, *least.*
Multus, *much.*	plus, *more.*	plus,	plurimus, *most.*
Nequam, (*in-decl.*), *bad.*	nequior, *worse.*	nequius,	nequissimus, *the worst.*

Obs. 1. *Plus*, gen. *pluris*, in the singular is only employed as a noun; in the plural it is also an adjective.

K

Obs. 2. *Juvenis,* young, has the comp. *junior;* *senex,* old, has *senior;* neither have any superlative.

EXCEPTION V.

The following adjectives have two irregular forms of the superlative.

Positive.	*Comp.*	*Superl.*
Exter,	exterior,	extremus *and* extimus,
outward.		*the extreme.*
Inferus,	inferior,	infimus *and* imus (*i* long),
inferior.		*the lowest.*
Superus,	superior,	supremus *and* summus,
superior.		*the highest.*
Posterus,	posterior,	postremus *and* postumus
posterior.	.	(*u* short), *hindmost.*

EXCEPTION VI.

Some comparatives and superlatives have no positive, and are derived from prepositions and adverbs.

Positive.	*Comp.*	*Superl.*
Citra,	citerior,	citimus,
on this side.	*more on this side.*	*the most on this side.*
Intra,	interior,	intimus,
within.	*interior.*	*the innermost.*
Præ,	prior,	primus,
before.	*the first of two.*	*the first.*
Ultra,	ulterior,	ultimus,
beyond.	*ulterior.*	*the last.*

Positive.	Comp.	Superl.
Deter,	deterior,	deterrimus,
(obsolete).	less good.	the least good.
Prope,	propior,	proximus,
near.	nearer.	the nearest.
Potis,	potior,	potissimus,
able.	abler.	the ablest.
From the	ocior,	ocissimus,
Gr. ὠκύς,	quicker.	the quickest.

EXCEPTION VII.

1. The following adjectives have no comparative:

Diversus, *divers.*	Novus, *new.*
Inclytus, *famous.*	Nuperus, *recent.*
Invictus, *invincible.*	Par, *even.*
Invitus, *forced.*	Sacer, *sacred.*

And also participles employed as adjectives:

Consultus, *understood.*	Persuasus, *persuaded.*
Meritus, *deserved.*	

2. The following have no superlative:

Adolescens, *young.*	Juvenis, *young.*
Agrestis, *uncultivated.*	Longinquus, *far.*
Alacer, *lively.*	Opimus, *rich.*
Arcanus, *secret.*	Proclivis, *inclined.*
Declivis, *inclining.*	Propinquus, *near.*
Deses, *lazy.*	Salutaris, *salutary.*
Diuturnus, *lengthy.*	Satur, *satisfied.*
Jejunus, *fasting.*	Senex, *old.*

Most of the adjectives in *alis, bilis, ilis* (*i* long), have no superlative.

Obs. As to those in *ilis* (*i* short), besides the six having the superlative in *illimus* (see above, Exception II.), the following are the only ones of which the superlative is in use :

Amabilis, *amiable.*	Ignobilis, *ignoble.*
Fertilis, *fertile.*	Mobilis, *changeable.*
Fragilis, *fragile.*	Sterilis, *sterile.*
Nobilis, *noble.*	Utilis, *useful.*

EXCEPTION VIII.

Adjectives ending in *us* preceded by a vowel do not take *ior* and *issimus* for their termination. The comparative and superlative are formed by placing the adverbs *magis*, more, and *maxime*, most, before them. Ex. :

Positive.	*Comp.*	*Superl.*
Idoneus,	magis idoneus,	maxime idoneus.
fit.		
Necessarius,	— necessarius,	— necessarius.
necessary.		
Arduus,	— arduus,	— arduus.
rugged.		

Obs. 1. Adjectives ending in *quus* and *guis* are only apparent exceptions to this rule. *Antiquus* has *antiquior* for the comparative, and *antiquissimus* for the superlative; *pinguis*, fat, *pinguior*, *pinguissimus*.

The real exceptions are : *assidúus, exiguus; strenuus*, vigorous ; *tenuis*, small, of which the comparative and superlative are often formed regularly : *assiduior, assiduissimus; strenuior, strenuissimus; tenuior, tenuissimus.*

Obs. 2. The comparative is often translated by "too " (more than is right) with the positive. Ex. : *difficilior*, too difficult ; *vehementior*, too vehement. The superlative is often translated by "very" with the positive. Ex. : *pulcherrimus*, very handsome.

B. *Declension of adjectives in the comparative and superlative.*

The comparative of adjectives is declined like adjectives having two terminations : the superlative like adjectives in *us, a, um.*

Observation.

a) The comparative does not take *ium* in the genitive plural, but *um*.

b) The neuter does not take *ia* in the nominative, vocative, or accusative plural, but *a*.

c) The ablative singular takes *e* rather than *i*.

EXAMPLE

OF THE DECLENSION OF A COMPARATIVE.

MASCULINE.

Singular.	*Plural.*
N. Doct*ior* magist*er*, a	N. Doct*iores* magist*ri*,
more learned master.	*more learned masters.*

Singular.	*Plural.*
G. Doctioris magistri, *of a more learned master.*	G. Doctiorum magistrorum, *of more learned masters.*
D. Doctiori magistro, *to a more learned master.*	D. Doctioribus magistris, *to more learned masters.*
A. Doctiorem magistrum, *a more learned master.*	A. Doctiores magistros, *more learned masters.*
V. ô Doctior magister, *o more learned master.*	V. ô Doctiores magistri, *o more learned masters.*
A. Doctiore magistro, *from or by a more learned master.*	A. Doctioribus magistris, *from or by more learned masters.*

FEMININE.

N. Felicior vita, *a happier life.*	N. Feliciores vitæ, *happier lives.*
G. Felicioris vitæ, *of a happier life.*	G. Feliciorum vitarum, *of happier lives.*
D. Feliciori vitæ, *to a happier life.*	D. Felicioribus vitis, *to happier lives.*
A. Feliciorem vitam, *a happier life.*	A. Feliciores vitas, *happier lives.*
V. ô Felicior vita, *o happier life.*	V. ô Feliciores vitæ, *o happier lives.*
A. Feliciore vita, *from or by a happier life.*	A. Felicioribus vitis, *from or by happier lives.*

NEUTER.

N. Clarius lumen, *a clearer light.*	N. Clariora lumina, *clearer lights.*
G. Clarioris luminis, *of a clearer light.*	G. Clariorum luminum, *of clearer lights.*

Singular.	Plural.
D. Clariori lumini, *to a clearer light.*	D. Clarioribus luminibus, *to clearer lights.*
A. Clarius lumen, *a clearer light.*	A. Clariora lumina, *clearer lights.*
V. ô Clarius lumen, *o clearer light.*	V. ô Clariora lumina, *o clearer lights.*
A. Clariore lumine, *from or by a clearer light.*	A. Clarioribus luminibus, *from or by clearer lights.*

EXAMPLE

OF THE DECLENSION OF A SUPERLATIVE.

MASCULINE.

N. Doctissimus magister, *a most learned master.*	N. Doctissimi magistri, *most learned masters.*
G. Doctissimi magistri, *of a most learned master.*	G. Doctissimorum magistrorum, *of most learned masters.*
D. Doctissimo magistro, *to a most learned master.*	D. Doctissimis magistris, *to most learned masters.*
A. Doctissimum magistrum, *a most learned master.*	A. Doctissimos magistros, *most learned masters.*
V. ô Doctissime magister, *o most learned master.*	V. ô Doctissimi magistri, *o most learned masters.*
A. Doctissimo magistro, *from or by a most learned master.*	A. Doctissimis magistris, *from or by most learned masters.*

FEMININE.

Singular.   *Plural.*

N. Felic*issima* vita, *the happiest life.*

N. Felic*issimæ* vitæ, *the happiest lives.*

G. Felic*issimæ* vitæ, *of the happiest life.*

G. Felic*issimarum* vita*rum, of the happiest lives.*

D. Felic*issimæ* vitæ, *to the happiest life.*

D. Felic*issimis* vitis, *to the happiest lives.*

A. Felic*issimam* vitam, *the happiest life.*

A. Felic*issimas* vitas, *the happiest lives.*

V. ô Felic*issima* vita, *o happiest life.*

V. ô Felic*issimæ* vitæ, *o happiest lives.*

A. Felic*issima* vita, *from* or *by the happiest life.*

A. Felic*issimis* vitis, *from* or *by the happiest lives.*

NEUTER.

N. Clar*issimum* lumen, *the clearest light.*

N. Clar*issima* lumina, *the clearest lights.*

G. Clar*issimi* luminis, *of the clearest light.*

G. Clar*issimorum* lumi*num, of the clearest lights.*

D. Clar*issimo* lumini, *to the clearest light.*

D. Clar*issimis* lumin*ibus, to the clearest lights.*

A. Clar*issimum* lumen, *the clearest light.*

A. Clar*issima* lumina, *the clearest lights.*

V. ô Clar*issimum* lumen, *o clearest light.*

V. ô Clar*issima* lumina, *o clearest lights.*

A. Clar*issimo* lumine, *from* or *by the clearest light.*

A. Clar*issimis* lumin*ibus, from* or *by the clearest lights.*

CHAPTER III.

DECLENSION OF PRONOUNS.

THERE are six kinds of pronouns:

      1. Personal pronouns.
      2. Possessive   ,,
      3. Demonstrative ,,
      4. Relative   ,,
      5. Interrogative ,,
      6. Indefinite   ,,

FIRST DIVISION.

PERSONAL PRONOUNS.

As the declension of pronouns shows every modification which these words undergo, it is essential to impress them on the memory. Therefore the pupil should compose a sort of scale of the cases of each pronoun. When the first and second persons sin-

gular are thus mastered, let him repeat them con-
secutively; and then proceed to the third person
masculine singular. When this is learnt, let the
three persons singular be repeated in the same way
as the two first, and so on with the rest, until the
personal pronouns be thoroughly learnt by heart.
Ex. :

	N.	G.	D.	A.	Ab.
1st pers. sing.	ego,	mei,	mihi,	me,	me.
2nd „ „	tu,	tui,	tibi,	te,	te.
3rd „ „	*is wanting,*	sui,	sibi,	se,	se [1].
1st pers. plur.	nos,	nostri *or* nostrum,	nobis,	nos,	nobis.
2nd „ „	vos,	vestri *or* vestrum,	vobis,	vos,	vobis.
3rd „ „	*is wanting,*	sui,	sibi,	se,	se.

When the pupil is able to repeat them thus by
heart, he must endeavour to repeat them with the
English translation.

	N.	G.	D.	A.	Ab.
1st pers. sing.	ego,	mei,	mihi,	me,	me,
	I,	*of me,*	*to me,*	*me,*	*from* or *by me.*
2nd „ „	tu,	tui,	tibi,	te,	te,
	thou,	*of thee,*	*to thee,*	*thee,*	*from* or *by thee.*
3rd „ „	*is wanting,*	sui,	sibi,	se,	se,
		of him- self,	*to him- self,*	*him- self,*	*from* or *by himself,*
		of her- self,	*to her- self,*	*her- self,*	or *her- self.*

---

[1] Properly speaking there is no personal pronoun of the third person
singular in Latin; the demonstrative and determining pronouns (p.
120, et seq.) supply its place when required.

	N.	G.	D.	A.	Ab.
1st pers. plur.	nos, *we,*	nostri *or* nostrum, *of us,*	nobis, *to us,*	nos, *us,*	nobis, *from* or *by us.*
2nd „ „	vos, *you,*	vestri *or* vestrum, *of you,*	vobis, *to you,*	vos, *you,*	vobis, *from* or *by you.*
3rd „ „	*is wanting,*	sui, *of them-selves,*	sibi, *to them-selves,*	se, *them-selves,*	se, *from* or *by them-selves.*

Obs. The pronoun of the third person is always a reflective pronoun; the first and second person may also be employed as such [2].

SECOND DIVISION.

POSSESSIVE PRONOUNS.

The possessive pronouns are derived from the personal pronouns: they have the form of adjectives in *us, a, um,* and are declined like them.

	M.	F.	N.
1st pers. sing.	meus,	mea,	meum, *my, mine.*
2nd „ „	tuus,	tua,	tuum, *thy, thine.*
3rd „ „	suus, *his.*	sua, *her.*	suum, *its.*

---

[2] They are then frequently followed by *met*, indeclinable, and by *metipse*, which is declinable.

	M.	*F.*	*N.*
1st pers. plur.	noster,	nostra,	nostrum, *our* or *ours.*
2nd „ „	vester,	vestra,	vestrum, *your* or *yours.*
3rd „ „	suus,	sua,	suum, *their* or *theirs.*

Obs. The third person of the possessive pronoun has no particular form to mark the number of the possessor.

The declension of the possessive pronouns being the same as that of adjectives in *us* (*er*), *a*, *um* (see p. 93), it is needless to repeat it here. It is sufficient to remark that the vocative masculine of *meus* is *mi*.

THIRD DIVISION.

DEMONSTRATIVE PRONOUNS.

There are two sorts:

a) Those expressing a relation of place with respect to the person who speaks.

b) Those which determine a person or a thing already named, and therefore known, or a person or a thing to which the relative pronoun belongs, which pronoun is then placed after them. For this reason they are called *determinative.*

A. Demonstrative pronouns expressing a relation of place are :

M.	F.	N.
Hic,	hæc,	hoc, *this, this one.*
Ille,	illa,	illud, *that, that one.*
Iste,	ista,	istud, *that, that other one.*

They are declined as follows :

Singular.

M.	F.	N.
N. Hic,	hæc,	hoc, *this, this one.*
G. Hujus (for the three genders), *of this,* &c.		
D. Huic (for the three genders), *to this,* &c.		
A. Hunc,	hanc,	hoc, *this,* &c.
A. Hoc,	hac,	hoc, *from this* or *by this,* &c.

Plural.

N. Hi,	hæ,	hæc, *these,* &c.
G. Horum,	harum,	horum, *of these,* &c.
D. His (for the three genders), *to these,* &c.		
A. Hos,	has,	hæc, *these.*
A. His (for the three genders), *from these* or *by these,* &c.		

Singular.

N. Ille,	illa,	illud, *that,* &c.
G. Illius (for the three genders), *of that,* &c.		
D. Illi (for the three genders), *to that,* &c.		
A. Illum,	illam,	illud, *that,* &c.
A. Illo,	illa,	illo, *from* or *by that,* &c.

L

Plural.

M.	F.	N.
N. Illi,	illæ,	illa, *those,* &c.
G. Illorum,	illarum,	illorum, *of those,* &c.

D. Illis (for the three genders), *to those,* &c.

| A. Illos, | illas, | illa, *those,* &c. |

A. Illis (for the three genders), *from* or *by those.*

Iste is declined like *ille.*

B. The determinative pronouns are :

Is,	ea,	id, *he, she, it, that.*
Idem,	eadem,	idem, *the same.*
Ipse,	ipsa,	ipsum, *myself, thyself, him* or *herself.*
Talis,		tale, *such,*	correlative of *qualis* and *quantus.* See relative and interrogative pronouns.
Tantus,	tanta,	tantum, *so much,*	

They are declined as follows :

Singular.

N. Is,	ea,	id, *he, she, it.*

G. Ejus (for the three genders), *of him, of her, of it.*

D. Ei (for the three genders), *to him, to her, to it.*

| A. Eum, | eam, | id, *him, her, it.* |
| A. Eo, | ea, | eo, *from* or *by him, her, it.* |

Plural.

M.	F.	N.
N. Ii,	eæ,	ea, *they.*
G. Eorum,	earum,	eorum, *of them.*

D. Iis *or* eis (for the three genders), *to them.*

| A. Eos, | eas, | ea, *them.* |

A. Iis *or* eis (for the three genders), *from them.*

Singular.

N. Idem,	eadem,	idem, *the same.*

G. Ejusdem (for the three genders), *of the same.*

D. Eidem (for the three genders), *to the same.*

A. Eumdem,	eamdem,	idem, *the same.*
A. Eodem,	eadem,	eodem, *from* or *by the*
		the same.

Plural.

N. Iidem,	eædem,	eadem, *the same.*
G. Eorumdem,	earumdem,	eorumdem, *of the same.*

D. Iisdem *or* eisdem (for the three genders), *to the same.*

| A. Eosdem, | easdem, | eadem, *the same.* |

A. Eisdem *or* iisdem (for the three genders), *from* or *by the same.*

Singular.

N. Ipse,	ipsa,	ipsum, *myself, thyself, himself, herself, itself.*

G. Ipsius (for the three genders), *of myself, thyself,* &c.

D. Ipsi (for the three genders), *to myself,* &c.

L 2

Singular.

M.	F.	N.
A. Ipsum,	ipsam,	ipsum, *myself*, &c.
A. Ipso,	ipsa,	ipso, *from* or *by my-self*, &c.

Plural.

N. Ipsi,	ipsæ,	ipsa, *ourselves, your-selves, themselves.*
G. Ipsorum,	ipsarum,	ipsorum, *of ourselves,*&c.
D. Ipsis (for the three genders), *to ourselves*, &c.		
A. Ipsos,	ipsas,	ipsa, *ourselves*, &c.
A. Ipsis (for the three genders), *from* or *by ourselves*, &c.		

Obs. Talis is declined like the adjectives ending in *is, e; tantus,* like those ending in *us, a, um.*

FOURTH DIVISION.

RELATIVE PRONOUNS.

They are:

Qui, quæ, quod, *who, that, which.*

Qualis, e, *such a one, such as.*

Quicunque, quæcunque, quodcunque, *which, whoever, whatever, whatsoever.*

Qualiscunque, *whoever, whatever, whichever.*

They are declined as follows:

Singular.

M.	F.	N.
N. Qui,	quæ,	quod, *who, which, that.*

G. Cujus (for the three genders), *of whom, of which.*

D. Cui (for the three genders), *to whom, to which.*

| A. Quem, | quam, | quod, *whom, which, that.* |
| A. Quo, | qua, | quo, *from* or *by whom, which, that.* |

Plural.

| N. Qui, | quæ, | quæ, *who, that, which.* |
| G. Quorum, | quarum, | quorum, *of whom, of that, of which.* |

D. Quibus (for the three genders), *to whom, to that, to which.*

| A. Quos, | quas, | quæ, *whom, that, which.* |

A. Quibus (for the three genders), *from* or *by whom, that, which.*

Obs. Qui is often used for *is qui,* he who, and *quod* for *id quod,* and in the plural *quæ* is employed rather than *ea quæ.* Ex.: *Bis vincit qui* (for *is qui*) *se vincit,* he doubly conquers who conquers himself. *Quod* (for *id quod*) *dicis non mihi placet,* what (that which) thou sayest does not please me.

Qualis, e, is only employed in conjunction with the demonstrative *talis.* It is declined like the adjectives in *is, e.*

Quicunque is declined like *qui,* the affix *cunque* always remains invariable.

FIFTH DIVISION.

INTERROGATIVE PRONOUNS.

They are as follows:

Quis? quid? *who? what?*

Qui, quæ, quod? *which?*

Qualis, e? *which? which sort of?*

Quis is used for the masculine and feminine, and *quid* for the neuter. It is an absolute or substantive interrogative pronoun.

Qui, quæ, quod, is a relative or adjective interrogative pronoun.

They are declined exactly like the relative pronouns.

SIXTH DIVISION.

INDEFINITE PRONOUNS.

They are as follows:

M.	F.	N.	
Quis,	(qua),	quid,	*some one.*
Qui,	quæ,	quod,	*some.*

They are declined like the relative pronoun, as are also their compounds:

1) Aliquis, aliqua, aliquid *and* aliquod, *some one, some.*

2) Quidam, quædam, quiddam (*or* quoddam), *some one, such a one.*

3) Quispiam, quæpiam, quidpiam (quodpiam), *some one, some.*

4) Quisquam, quidquam, *some* or *any one, some* or *any thing.*

5) Quisque, quæque, quidque (quodque), *each, every one.*

6) Quivis, quævis, quidvis (quodvis), *whosoever, whoever he, she, it may be.*

7) Quilibet, quælibet, quidlibet (quodlibet), *whosoever, whichever.*

8) Quicunque, quæcunque, quodcunque, *any one.*

9) Quisquis, quidquid, *whosoever, whichever.*

They are declined like *quis* and *qui*, the affix remaining invariable. *Quisquis* alone declines both its component words; but the genitive is *cuicui* (instead of *cujuscujus*); accusative, *quemquem, quidquid,* &c.

Obs. When these pronouns are employed as adjectives, they have the neuter *quod* instead of *quid.* Ex.: *aliquid,* something; *aliquod oraculum,* some oracle.

We must add to this division the following pronominal adjectives:

Unus, *one.*	Neuter, *neither of two.*
Ullus, *some.*	Solus, *only, alone.*
Nullus, *none.*	Totus, *all.*
Uter, *which of two.*	Alius, *other* (neut. *aliud*).
Alter, *one of two.*	

And their compounds :

Unusquisque, *each.*

Uterque, *both.*

Utervis, *whichever of the two.*

Alteruter, *either.*

They are declined like the adjectives in *us* (*er*), *a*, *um*, except in the genitive and dative singular, which like the pronouns have only one form for the three genders, viz., *ius* (*i* long) in the genitive, and *i* in the dative.

As an example we give the declension of the following :

	M.	*F.*	*N.*
N.	Un*us*,	un*a*,	un*um*, *one.*
G.	Un*ius* (for the three genders).		
D.	Un*i* (for the three genders).		
A.	Un*um*,	un*am*,	un*um*.
A.	Un*o*,	un*a*,	un*o*.

Obs. 1. *Alius* is the only one of which the neuter ends in *ud, aliud.*

Obs. 2. In the compounds *unusquisque, uterque, utervis, alteruter,* we decline the part that is declinable ; thus *unusquisque* will become:

N. Unusquisque, unaquæque, unumquidque, *each.*

G. Uniuscujusque, *of each.*

D. Unicuique, *to each,* &c.

There are two ways of declining *alteruter :* in the

feminine it becomes *altera utra,* and in the neuter *alterum utrum,* and consequently in the genitive *alterius utrius;* or else *uter* only is declined: the feminine then is *alterutra,* the neuter *alterutrum,* the genitive *alterutrius,* &c.

Obs. 3. *Uterque,* both, only admits of the plural when it relates to two opposite objects, each containing a plural idea. Thus *uterque exercitus* means both armies; *utrumque oppidum,* both towns; but *utrique Macedones et Tyrii* means, both the Macedonians and the Tyrians.

ANALYTICAL INDEX

OF THE

CONTENTS OF THIS VOLUME.

GILBERT AND RIVINGTON, PRINTERS, ST. JOHN'S SQUARE, LONDON.

A SELECTION OF WORKS,

PUBLISHED BY

WHITTAKER AND CO., AVE MARIA LANE.

	£	s.	d.
ANTHON'S VIRGIL. Adapted for the Use of English Schools, by the Rev. F. METCALFE. With Notes at the end. 12mo. cloth	0	7	6
BAIRD'S Classical Manual. 12mo. cloth	0	4	0
BEATSON'S Progressive Exercises on the Composition of Greek Iambic Verse. 12mo. cloth	0	3	0
BELLENGER'S French Conversations. New edition. 12mo. cloth	0	2	6
BIBLIOTHECA CLASSICA:—			
ÆSCHYLUS. With a Commentary, by F. A. PALEY, M.A.	0	18	0
CICERO'S ORATIONS. Edited by G. LONG, M.A. 4 vols. 8vo. cloth. (The volumes sold separately)	3	4	0
DEMOSTHENES. With a Commentary, by the Rev. R. WHISTON, M.A. Vol. I. 8vo. cloth	0	16	0
EURIPIDES. With a Commentary, by F. A. PALEY, M.A. Vols. I., II. & III. Sold separately. 8vo. cloth, each	0	16	0
HERODOTUS. With English Notes, &c., by the Rev. J. W. BLAKESLEY, B.D. 2 vols. 8vo. cloth	1	12	0
HESIOD. With English Notes, by F. A. PALEY, M.A. 8vo. cloth	0	10	6
HORACE. With a Commentary, by the Rev. A. J. MACLEANE. 8vo. cloth	0	18	0
JUVENAL and PERSIUS. With a Commentary, by the Rev. A. J. MACLEANE. 8vo. cloth	0	14	0
SOPHOCLES. With a Commentary, by the Rev. F. H. M. BLAYDES, M.A. Vol. I. 8vo. cloth	0	18	0
TERENCE. With a Commentary, by the Rev. E. ST. JOHN PARRY. 8vo. cloth	0	18	0
VIRGIL. Vol. I. Containing the Eclogues and Georgics. With a Commentary, by J. CONINGTON, M.A. 8vo. cloth	0	12	0
⁎ Other volumes will shortly be published.			
BOYER and DELETANVILLE'S Complete French Dictionary. New edition. 8vo. bound	0	12	0
BOYES'S (Rev. J. F.) English Repetitions in Prose and Verse. 12mo. cloth	0	3	6
BUTTMANN'S (Dr. P.) Intermediate, or Larger Greek Grammar. New edit., by Dr. CHAS. SUPF. 8vo. cloth	0	12	0
BYTHNER'S Lyre of David. By the Rev. T. DEE, A.B. New edition, by N. L. BENMOHEL, A.M. 8vo. cloth	1	4	0
CÆSAR de Bello Gallico. With English Notes, &c., by GEORGE LONG, M.A. 12mo. cloth	0	5	6
CAMPAN'S (Madame) Conversations in *French and English.* New edition. 12mo. cloth	0	3	6
—————————— in *German and English.* 12mo. cloth	0	4	0
CHEPMELL'S (Rev. Dr. H. Le M.) Course of History. First Series. 12mo. cloth	0	5	0
—————————— Second Series. 2 vols. 12mo. cloth	0	12	0
—————————— Questions on the First Series. 12mo. sewed	0	1	0
CICERO'S Minor Works. De Officiis, &c. &c. With English Notes, by W. C. TAYLOR, LL.D. 12mo. cloth	0	4	6

	£	s.	d.
CICERO de Amicitia, de Senectute, &c. With Notes, &c., by G. Long, Esq., M.A. 12mo. cloth	0	4	6
COMSTOCK'S System of Natural Philosophy. New edition, by Lees. 18mo. bound	0	3	6
DAWSON'S Greek-English Lexicon to the New Testament. New edition, by Dr. Taylor. 8vo. cloth	0	9	0
DES CARRIERE, Histoire de France. Par C. J. Delille. 12mo. bound	0	7	0
DRAKENBORCH'S LIVY, Crevier's Notes, 3 vols. 8vo. cl.	1	11	6
EURIPIDES (Porson's). New edition, with Notes from Schaefer and others. 8vo. cloth	0	10	6
₊ The four Plays separate. 8vo. sewed, each	0	2	6
FLUGEL'S German and English, and English and German Dictionary. New edition. 2 vols. 8vo. cloth	1	4	0
————— Abridged. 12mo. bound	0	7	6
FOREIGN CLASSICS. 12mo. cloth:—			
CHARLES XIIth, by Direy	0	3	6
FONTAINE'S FABLES, by Gase	0	3	0
PICCIOLA, SAINTINE, by Dubuc	0	3	0
SCHILLER'S WALLENSTEIN, by Buchheim	0	6	6
TELEMAQUE, FENELON, by Delille	0	4	6
GRADUS ad PARNASSUM. Pyper. New and improved edition. 12mo. cloth	0	7	0
GREEK TESTAMENT (The). With Notes, &c., by the Rev. J. F. Macmichael, B.A. 12mo. cloth	0	7	6
HAMEL'S New Universal French Grammar. New edition. 12mo. bound	0	4	0
————— French Exercises. New edition. 12mo. bound	0	4	0
₊ Key to ditto. New edition. 12mo. bound	0	3	0
————— French Grammar and Exercises, by Lambert. 12mo. bound	0	5	6
₊ Key to ditto, by Lambert. 12mo. bound	0	4	0
HEALE'S (Rev. E. M.) Manual of Geography for the Use of Military Students. 12mo. cloth	0	4	6
HINCKS' Greek and English School Lexicon. New edition, improved. square, bound	0	7	6
————— Summary of Ancient and Modern History. New edition. 18mo. cloth	0	3	0
HISTORICAL EPITOME of the Old and New Testaments, by a Member of the Church of England. 12mo. bound	0	6	0
HOBLYN'S Dictionary of Medical Terms. New edition, much enlarged. sm. 8vo. cloth	0	12	6
HORACE. With English Notes, by the Rev. A. J. Macleane, M.A. Abridged. 12mo. cloth	0	6	6
HOSE'S Elements of Euclid. With New and Improved Diagrams. 12mo. cloth	0	4	6
JUVENALIS SATIRÆ XVI. With English Notes, by H. Prior, M.A. 12mo. cloth	0	4	6
KEIGHTLEY'S History of India. 8vo. cloth	0	8	0
KOCH'S History of Europe. 8vo. cloth	0	6	0
LEBAHN'S Practice in German. 12mo. cloth	0	6	0
LE BRETON'S French Scholar's First Book. 12mo. cl.	0	3	0

£ s. d.

LEVIZAC'S French Dictionary. New edit. 12mo. bound 0 6 6
LIVY. English Notes, by Dr. STOCKER. 4 vols. 8vo. bds. 2 8 0
LONG'S (George, M.A.) Atlas of Classical Geography.
    With copious Index, &c. 8vo. half-bound . . . 0 12 6
    ——————————— Grammar School Atlas of Classical
    Geography. 8vo. cloth 0 5 0

MOORE'S Dictionary of Quotations. 8vo. cloth . . 0 12 0

MORRISON'S (C.) System of Practical Book-keeping by
    Single and Double Entry. New edition. 8vo. half-bd. 0 8 0

NIBLOCK'S Latin-English and English-Latin Dictionary.
    square 12mo. bound 0 9 0

OLLENDORFF'S (Dr. H. G.) French Method. New
    edition. 8vo. cloth 0 12 0
    ₊ Key to ditto, by Dr. OLLENDORFF. 8vo. cloth . 0 7 0
    ——————————————————————— School
    edition. 12mo. cloth 0 6 6
    ——————— German Method. Part I. New
    edition. 8vo. cloth 0 12 0
    ——————————————————— Part II. New
    edition. 8vo. cloth 0 12 0
    ₊ Key to ditto (both parts). 8vo. cloth . . 0 7 0
    ——————— Introductory Book to his German
    Method. 12mo. cloth 0 3 6
    ——————— Italian Method. New edit. 8vo. cloth 0 12 0
    ₊ Key to ditto, by Dr. OLLENDORFF. 8vo. cloth . 0 7 0
    ——————— Spanish Method. 8vo. cloth . 0 12 0
    ₊ Key to ditto, by Dr. OLLENDORFF. 8vo. cloth . 0 7 0
OVID'S FASTI. With English Notes, &c., by F. A.
    PALEY, M.A. 12mo. cloth 0 5 0

WHITTAKER'S IMPROVED EDITIONS OF

PINNOCK'S History of England. New and revised edition.
    12mo. bound roan 0 6 0
    ——————— Rome. New edit. 12mo. bd. roan 0 5 6
    ——————— Greece. New edit. 12mo. bd. roan 0 5 6
    ——————— Arithmetical Tables. 18mo. sewed. New edit. 0 0 6
    ——————— Ciphering Book. No. 1. Fcap. 4to. swd. . 0 1 0
    ——————————————— No. 2. Fcap. 4to. hf.-bd. . 0 3 0
    ——————— Key to Ciphering Books. 12mo. bound . 0 3 6
    ——————— Child's First Book. 18mo. sewed . 0 0 3
    ——————— Explanatory English Reader. 12mo. bound . 0 4 6
    ——————— Introduction to ditto. 12mo. cloth . 0 3 0
    ——————— English Spelling Book. New edit. 12mo. cloth 0 1 6
    ——————— Exercises in False Spelling. 18mo. cloth . 0 1 6
    ——————— First Spelling Book. 18mo. cloth . . 0 1 0
    ——————— Juvenile Reader. 12mo. cloth . . 0 1 6
    ——————— Mentorian Primer. 18mo. half-bound . 0 0 6
    ——————— (W. H.) First Latin Grammar. Ollendorff's
    system. 12mo. cloth 0 3 0
    ——————— Catechisms of the Arts and Sciences. 12 vols.
    18mo. cloth 3 12 0
    ₊ Separately, 18mo. sewed . . . . each 0 0 9

	£	s.	d.
PENROSE'S (Rev. John) Easy Exercises in Latin Elegiac Verse. New edition. 12mo. cloth	0	2	0
PLATO'S APOLOGY. With Latin Version, by STANFORD. 8vo. cloth	0	10	6
PLATT'S Literary and Scientific Class Book. New and revised edition. 12mo. bound	0	5	0
SALLUST. With English Notes, by GEORGE LONG, M.A. 12mo. cloth	0	5	0
SECRETARY'S (The) Assistant. New edition. 18mo. cl.	0	2	6
SHAKESPEARE. Edited by J. PAYNE COLLIER, Esq. With Portrait and Vignette. Super-royal 8vo. cloth	1	1	0
SOPHOCLES, by MITCHELL. With English Notes, Critical and Explanatory. 2 vols. 8vo. cloth	1	8	0
⁎ The Plays can be had separately. 8vo. cloth . each	0	5	0
STODDART'S New Delectus ; or, Easy Steps to Latin Construing. 12mo. cloth	0	4	0
TACITUS. Germania and Agricola. With English Notes, by the Rev. P. FROST. 12mo. cloth	0	3	6
TAYLOR'S (Dr. W. C.) History of France and Normandy. 12mo. bound	0	6	0
———— History of the Overthrow of the Roman Empire. 12mo. cloth	0	6	6
TYTLER'S Elements of Universal History, with continuation. 8vo. cloth	0	4	6
VALPY'S GRADUS, Latin and English. New edition. royal 12mo. bound	0	7	6
———— Greek Testament, for Schools. New edition. 12mo. bound	0	5	0
———— SALLUST. New edition. 12mo. cloth	0	2	6
———— With English Notes, by HICKIE. 12mo. cloth	0	4	6
———— Cornelius NEPOS. New edition. 12mo. cloth	0	2	6
———— With English Notes, by HICKIE. 12mo. cloth	0	3	6
———— Schrevelius's Greek and English Lexicon. New edition, by Dr. MAJOR. 8vo. cloth	0	10	6
VENERONI'S Italian Grammar. New edit. 12mo. bound	0	6	0
WALKER'S DICTIONARY. Remodelled by SMART. New edition. 8vo. cloth	0	12	0
———— Epitomized by ditto. 12mo. cloth	0	6	0
WALKINGAME'S Tutor's Assistant. By FRASER. New edition. 12mo. cloth	0	2	0
⁎ Key to ditto. New edition. 12mo. cloth	0	3	0
WEBER'S Outlines of Universal History. Translated by Dr. M. BEHR. 8vo. cloth	0	9	0
WHITTAKER'S Florilegium Poeticum. 18mo. cloth	0	3	0
———— Latin Exercises ; or, Exempla Propria. 12mo. cloth	0	3	0
WILLIAMS'S (Rev. D.) Preceptor's Assistant. 12mo. bd.	0	5	0
XENOPHON'S Anabasis. With English Notes, &c., by the Rev. J. F. MACMICHAEL, B.A. 12mo. cloth	0	5	0
———— Cyropædia. With English Notes, by the Rev. G. M. GORHAM, M.A. 12mo. cloth	0	6	0

Lightning Source UK Ltd.
Milton Keynes UK
UKHW020734140922
408851UK00005B/563